C_c
LOVI

"This is how we make the best environmentalists-by teaching people to fall in love with their places. For it is the love of place that inspires the deepest and most sustainable actions on behalf of the earth. I highly recommend this passionate and engaging love story."
—Jed Swift, MA, Director, Ecopsychology Program, Naropa University

"An inspiring book that brings back the best memories of first love. The book re-awakened me to all the wild things and places that—amidst long 'to do' lists—I don't have time to directly experience anymore, and it made me want to reclaim them as part of my life. The essays are a testament to the fact that we all need to return to the roots of our first love and renew our love affair with Nature."
—Dr. Gabriela Chavarria, Natural Resources Defense Council

"The 'Millennial Generation,' larger in size than even the Baby Boomers, is inside and plugged-in, raising the specter that America could lose a generation of outdoor enthusiasts. We're at risk of losing our collective inner voices, diminished, but crying out the psychological, physiological, and spiritual call of nature. *"Courting the Wild..."* surfaces and gathers elegantly the passionate enunciations of everyday people with cathartic personal realizations that *out* there is, inextricably and rewardingly, *in* all of us."
—Mickey Freeman, Chief Operating Officer, Outward Bound, Inc.

"Full of bustle and busy-ness, today's 'modern' societies leave people roaming from cafe to club to computer in search of love. *Courting the Wild* reminds us that love is available to each of us, every day, in our natural surroundings—the ancient, innate, and healing love experienced through re-connecting with nature. The book's blissful accounts illustrate how for each of us, there is a natural place where we can go to escape the stressful noise of our go, go, go, society—to find the quiet that we need to hear the guiding voice of our heart whispering into our soul what direction to take next."

—Dr. Jon Gelbard, Executive Director, Conservation Value Institute and National Sustainability Producer, Green Apple Festival

Courting the Wild
LOVE AFFAIRS WITH THE LAND

James B. Reason

Courting the Wild
LOVE AFFAIRS WITH THE LAND

Edited by
Jamie K. Reaser &
Susan Chernak McElroy

HIRAETH PRESS
DANVERS, MASSACHUSETTS

Cover design by Jason Kirkey
Cover photograph © iStockphoto.com /Andreas Gäbler
Back photograph © iStockphoto.com / Lorenzo Puricelli

ISBN: 978-0-9799246-3-7

Recommended citation:
Reaser, Jamie K. and Chernak McElroy, Susan. *Courting the
Wild: Love Affairs with the Land.* Danvers, Mass.: Hiraeth
Press, 2008.

Published by Hiraeth Press
Danvers, Massachusetts
www.hiraethpress.com

This book is lovingly dedicated to
Gaia
and all those who honor her.

CONTENTS

ACKNOWLEDGEMENTS

Our sincere gratitude to those who have helped birth this project: first and foremost our thanks go to all of the essay contributors who shared their personal stories. We greatly appreciate their open hearts, as well as their diligence and patience throughout the editorial process. Frank Owen deserves special recognition for his contributions to the original vision of the book and for assistance in editing some of the first manuscript submissions. Linda-Lu Misa, Rebecca Blanco, Tina Fields, Marlow Shami, and Jill Wicknick helped expand the resources section. Jason Kirkey graciously stepped into the role of "midhusband," guiding the delivery of the book into tangible reality through Hiraeth Press. We are ever so thankful for your gifts our brother.

INTRODUCTION

Embracing the Whole of
Nature and Our Humanity

A human being is a part of the whole called by us "the universe," a part limited in time and space. He experiences himself, his thoughts and feelings, as something separate from the rest a kind of optical delusion of consciousness. This delusion is a kind of prison for us, restricting us to our personal desires and affection for a few persons nearest to us. Our task must be to free ourselves from this prison by widening the circle of understanding and compassion to embrace all living creatures and the whole of nature in its beauty.

- Albert Einstein

Do you remember the first time you fell in love? Was it with a forest, a meadow, a hidden glen in your own backyard, or perhaps, a gently cascading creek? In what way are you and your first love still courting?

What do the places each of us love have in common? What empowers such places to evoke a mood and a memory? Why is it that a particular configuration of waters, stones, herbs, wildlife, branches, weather, and history has the ability to transform us into better people? This collection of essays is an invitation to explore these soul-centric questions through the voices of people who have also been smitten with place.

Within these pages you will find love stories, rapturous love affairs with the land, longings, shameless seductions, betrothals, vows exchanged, marriages of the soul, heartaches, partings, healings, and renewals. The authors are the courters and the courted. They are teachers and students, scientists and shamans, psychologists and poets, druids and activists, business leaders and bus drivers. Their landscape paramours embrace them and they grow forth from within.

Here too you will find the offspring of these love affairs: the birth of environmental stewardship and the rebirth of the human psyche.

Indeed, it is our task as humans "to free ourselves from this prison (of isolation) by widening the circle of understanding and compassion to embrace all living creatures and the whole of nature in its beauty." Furthermore, it is our privileged duty to work to sustain the heart-opening, soul-nurturing land that sustains us. Nothing else can, or will.

Let each author take you by hand and guide you on journey away from closed spaces and the maddening rush of the technological world. You will find yourself invited into a gentle exploration of places, life experiences, and tender dream-like reflections.

We hope that in reading these stories and engaging in the practices that follow each one, you will find the compass, map, and territory for your own love affair with the land. We encourage you to evolve your own earth-honoring traditions and to adopt them as a way of being. To build an intimate connection with the land is to foster a relationship with one's own unique and complex humanity. Thus, ultimately, we hope that you will find ways to acknowledge and celebrate your own true nature as a part of the whole called by us "the universe."

And, we hope that you will share your passion. We encourage conservation educators, wilderness guides, social marketers, ecopsychologists, and spiritual leaders of all traditions to use these stories and practices as a resource. Feel free to recite them in group formats.

May your love affair with the land be as enduring as a rock, as magnificent as mountain view, and as flowing as a stream. And, may you tread softly throughout your journey.

Jamie K. Reaser,
Blue Ridge Mountains,
Virginia

Susan Chernak McElroy,
the hill country,
southern Indiana

ECOS:
THE TRANSFORMATIVE LOVE OF PLACE

Frank Owen

An ancient rock shelf in western Ireland.
A bubbling blue stone well in the Catskills.
A misty Shinto shrine in northern Colorado.
The cacophony of crickets in a cyprus swamp along the Natchez Trace in Mississippi.
A gurgling spring rising straight out of Scottish earth.
An ice-cold forest pool in the Ozark foothills of Missouri.

These are some of the places that stir emotion within me. In contemplating the love of place, the spirit of place, and charged with the task of giving some form and shape to *my* love affair with the land, I quickly realized that there is no singular place that bears the weight of my affections, my attractions, my longing. In effect, when it comes to loving the land I am something of an "eco-harlot;" I am as promiscuous as they come.

Put another way, similar to the many women I have known and courted in my life, I have fallen in love many times with many places. Each of these places, with their distinct aromas, their vibrant light, their graceful curves, the "voice" of their waters, and their unyielding capacity to intoxicate me, has led me to a simple, yet profound, conclusion. Not unlike women—who are each goddesses in their own unique way—each place, *every* place, has the potential of leading us into an experience of expanded senses, deepening our awareness, and awakening within us an unbridled admiration for a location.

I've been blessed to have many relationships with sacred sites, beautiful places, landscapes of natural wonderment. There was, however, a first—a time and a place when and where I experienced the nascent stirrings of love for the land…what we might call *Ecos* rather than *Eros*.

Imagine a stretch of old growth forest. Yellow poplar. White oak. Black oak. Northern red oak. Hickory. See large boulders pushing their way up through moss-covered earth. A fox scampers into a fern meadow. A kingsnake slithers across the ground and into a hollow made by the marriage of flint splinters and oak roots. A raccoon peers down from a hole twenty feet off the ground in a large pine tree. A late spring breeze blows through the forest. White dogwood blossoms tremor on branches like dancing stars.

Such was the view from the back porch of my childhood home in Atlanta, Georgia, the day that I *consciously* fell in love with the land. We lived at the end of cul-de-sac, nestled up against a rich, green canopy of trees. It was not a rural area, per se, but a few steps into the woods behind that creaky old house and the look and feel of the land made it seem as if you were hiking in the remote mountains of northern Georgia.

If you traveled less than half a mile in any direction, you would encounter civilization: railroad tracks to the west, Toco Hills shopping center to the north, a major thoroughfare to the east, and Emory University to the south. But to my six-year-old sensibilities, the forest behind our home was a wild place of mystery and discovery. The adult world did not belong there. In my mind's eye, those woods were the domain of magical beings, "night creatures," and even Indians. But, of course, all of that is true.

Long before it became the thriving metropolis of Atlanta, the land was home to the Muskogee (Creek) and Eastern Tsalagi (Cherokee). Small tribal bands of Native American peoples had moved into the area nearly ten thousand years before. Over time, sophisticated Mississippian civilizations bearing corn agriculture established their presence in what has come to be known as the Southern Piedmont. It was here that these ancient peoples erected palisade villages and ceremonial mounds, many of which can still be seen across Georgia, Alabama, Mississippi, and Louisiana. Explorer

Hernando de Soto traveled across the Southern Piedmont range in the mid-1500s and recorded his impressions of these remarkable cities in his journals.

In 1821, these same lands were ceded to the State of Georgia by the Etowah Cherokee and the Middle Creek people, and under the swift pen of President Andrew Jackson, the so-called "Five Civilized Tribes" were forcibly removed to "Indian Territory" in Oklahoma; a deadly march that would come to be known as "The Trail of Tears." Forty-three years later, in 1864, following a Union victory at the Battle of Chattanooga, General William Tecumseh Sherman would pay a visit to this area and burn it to the ground in his infamous "March to the Sea."

On June 25, 1908, the area officially became known as "Druid Hills" by the DeKalb County Superior Court. No one knows exactly why this name was selected for this part of the Piedmont. My own working theory is that something about the old growth forests and the mists that frequent the woods in early spring and fall triggered something archetypal in the psyche of European descendents. Mist. Ancient trees. Druids. It makes perfect sense.

The Druid Hills area attracted some of Atlanta's wealthiest and most influential families, including the Candlers—owners of Coca-Cola—whom Emory University's Candler School of Theology is named for. Asa Candler, who received the original charter for the area from the Dekalb County Superior Court, is known to have headed the Druid Hills Corporation and shaped the community into an exclusive residential district. She not only oversaw strict building codes for residences, but also painstakingly sought to preserve the natural wonder of the area. Today Druid Hills is recognized on the National Register of Historic Places.

* * *

My first love affair with the land came one spring day in Druid Hills. It was a Saturday. For some reason, on this particular day, I skipped my most sacrosanct ritual of morning cartoons and headed straight into the woods. I informed my mother that I was "going on an expedition," to "chart the territory for those who would follow in my footsteps." My mother played along with my fantasy-game and made me a small pack lunch. My father made sure to impress upon me that if my "expedition ran out of supplies" that I could return to "base camp."

The morning was cool—a slight chill in the air kissed my skin. Droplets of mist settled upon my checks and eyelashes. Typically, when I explored these woods as a child, I would venture down about fifty yards into the trees, and I would stop at a certain grove, at a specific tree. It was "my tree," a "protector," a haven, a place of wonderment in the terrain of my childhood mysticism.

I had never ventured any further into the woods. Although I might have claimed that I was being a good boy and attending to parental requests that I keep the back of our old house in sight, in all honesty, the real motivating factor for staying next to "my tree" was fear. Total fear. I was afraid of the forest beyond, and my fear had a source.

At night, I would sometimes sit out on the screen porch and I would hear all manner of sounds coming from the dark woods around us. My imagination would run wild. Snapping twigs. Hissings. The flap of wings. The haunting thunderous rumble of trains-on-tracks from the other side of the wood. The occasional howling of *I-knew-not-what*. The shriek of small creatures coming to an untimely end. That forest was not just a stand of trees in my childhood psyche it was another world; two worlds in fact—one that appeared to be soft and welcoming by day, and another place that became haunted with unknowns as soon as the torch of day was snuffed out.

But this particular day, I walked beyond the familiar. My feet took me into the uncharted territory that I was convinced was the domain of strange creatures with large fangs.

Despite the presence of daylight I could easily conjure the images of all the dreaded creatures that my fears had crafted while I porch sat at night. Yet, something pushed me to walk deeper into the woods. Or, perhaps, like the Siren's call of ancient myth, something beckoned me, lulled me, drew me ever nearer.

Something did come over me. Rather than gallivanting through the trees as I might "playing cowboys and Indians," I moved at a snail's pace, taking in every tiny detail of every leaf, every rock, every insect.

My morning slowly flowed into afternoon.

Afternoon gradually faded into dusk.

With the dusk I began to observe the first signs of impending summer: the blinking strobe of lightning bugs.

I stood in wonderment, observing the day-forest give itself up to the night. As the energy of night began to take hold, I realized that by having spent the entire day in the woods of Druid Hills even *I* had been initiated into night. *I* was just as much a part of the night forest as all of the teeming life I could hear skittering through the leaves. I felt my heart open to the place. I felt such kinship with everything around me, and such gratitude that this special place existed. That day, I felt the place open to me as well. I had no language to describe it, only a deep sense that I was welcome and that I was, in fact, safe.

As I stood there, awash in the jungle-like sounds of the dark wood, I could feel a sensation begin to spin within me, though it was quite subtle at first. This sensation started as a basic appreciation for the place. The smell of the earth. The flickering of lightning bugs all around me. The cyclical rising and falling of the evening breeze, and how all of the sounds of the forest seemed to change with the breeze. It was as if everything were breathing, together, as one body.

Slowly, the subtle appreciation I felt for the place expanded. It expanded within me and, at the same time, felt as if it expanded *me*. I no longer felt like a stranger, nor was I an outside explorer on an "expedition." Instead, all at once, I felt a feeling of having merged into a union with the land. I truly felt *of* the place, intimate and deeply bound.

I suddenly ached with an emotion I had only associated with parents, grandparents, friends, and perhaps with a few pets. I felt love. Love for the place. Love for how the place caused me to feel. I felt *in* love, and I felt that the place loved me in return. The forest had always been vast and ominous to me before that day and night of deep communion, yet my love for the land had transformed my fear. This love caused me—just as any true love does—to feel bigger and better than I was before.

Though "my" tree still stands, that magical forest in Druid Hills is no longer there. It has since been bulldozed to the ground to make room for condominiums and university housing. Nonetheless, even now as an adult I can feel tenderness well up within me when I think of the place. It will always be the *axis mundi* in the mandala of my life at which my path of conscious spiritual awareness began.

Running like a thread throughout the journey of my life thus far (regardless of the different spiritual traditions or cultural forms I have explored) has been a core practice that runs backward through time to that special place. I never thought of it before now, but I'll simply call it *heart-opening*. Whether in the fern-filled valleys of the Trossachs in Scotland, the luscious jungles of Costa Rica, or on a quiet path within a Mississippi pine forest, I open my heart to the spirit of place, allowing the look, feel, sound, and energy to work its love-spell over me.

Frank Owen is an old soul passing through, currently leading a double life. By day he is a project manager and copywriter for an advertising and creative firm; by night, he is a "psychonavigational archaeologist" exploring transpersonal consciousness and the collective unconscious with the aid of a variety of ancient and post-modern tools. Under a nom de plume, he authored three books exploring Irish nature spirituality and shamanic states of consciousness—*The Mist-Filled Path*, *The Spiral of Memory and Belonging*, and *The Celtic Way of Seeing*. He can be reached via e-mail at: zenwhisky@ mac.com

PRACTICE:
LISTENING TO THE NIGHT SOUNDS

- Dress appropriately for the weather so that you can remain comfortable in the out-of-doors for an hour or more.
- Bring a flashlight for safety and a cushion or chair to sit on if you so choose. You might also want to bring a pen and journal for recording your observations.
- Go to a safe, outside location sometime after sunset. This location might be just a few steps away from your home or miles away from any signs of civilization.
- Sit down, turn off your flashlight, and allow your thoughts to become still (give yourself at least a few minutes to calm your mind).
- Option: practice "*Connecting with Nature*," page 55.
- Listen to the sounds of the night—sounds made by the natural elements (wind, for example) and their interactions with the land, those made by animals, and the sounds generated by human activity. Notice the sound of your own breath.
- Explore your response to these sounds: What images form in your mind's eye? What stories does your mind create about the sounds? What emotions do they stir? How are you affected by the direction, distance, volume, and presumed source of the sound?
- Journal your observations either on-site or soon after your return home.
- Repeat this practice regularly and in different locations. Notice how your observations change with time of night, location, and the associated characteristics of the sounds.

PRACTICE:
MAKING FRIENDS WITH THE DARK

- Dress appropriately for the weather so that you can remain comfortable in the out-of-doors for the entire night.

- Bring a flashlight for safety; adequate supply of water; a cushion or chair to sit on if you so choose; a pen and journal for recording your observations; a drum, rattle, or other percussion instrument(s); and a hand trowel and biodegradable or removable amenities should you need to use the "bathroom." Depending on the weather, you might also want to bring a sleeping bag and/or tarp and cords.

- Go to a safe, outside location soon after sunset. Choose a location that is, or at least seems to be, miles away from other human activity (e.g., it is absent street and building lights and traffic sounds, and you are unlikely to come across anyone else during your all night vigil).

- Choose a specific location to sit in for the night and set up your temporary "camp" as necessary so as to secure your comfort and safety.

- Sit down, turn off your flashlight, and allow your thoughts to become still (give yourself at least a few minutes to calm your mind).

- Recommendation: Practice *"Connecting with Nature,"* page 55.

- Listen to the sounds of the night—sounds made by the natural elements (wind, for example) and their inter-actions with the land, those made by animals, and the sounds generated by human activity. Notice the sound of your own breath.

- Explore your response to these sounds: What images form in your mind's eye? What stories does your mind create about the sounds? What emotions do they stir? How are you affected by the direction, distance, volume, and presumed source of the sound?

- If particular, pay attention to any sounds that stir fear or anxiety within you. What is the nature of these sounds what are their characteristics?
- Invite these sounds to be a guide for you. Notice what images and memories they stir. Notice where in your body your experience your reactions and place a hand on this location while applying light pressure.
- Do the sounds bring up fears or anxieties—ones formed as a child or an adult? What beliefs do they bring up about yourself and the world?
- Allow yourself to look at these fears/anxieties/beliefs as if you were watching them in front of your like a movie. Notice how certain sounds change the movie.
- Journal your observations.
- Pick up your percussion instrument and make your own sound (refrain from playing a song that you know, but rather let your feelings in the moment guide your beat) thus introducing yourself to all that is in the night.
- Notice how you feel letting the night creatures know of your presence.
- With your percussion instrument, communicate to the darkness (and in particular any of the "dark emotions" that it has evoked) that you wish to befriend it.
- Journal your observations.
- Repeat the process of listening, exploring your reactions, and setting the intent to befriend the darkness until sunrise.
- At sunrise, make an offering to the place for supporting your work there. You might offer some water, a song, a poem, personal story, prayer ties (see page 132), etc.
- Repeat this practice regularly and in different locations, inviting the night to take you deeper and deeper through layers of "internal darkness."

- Notice how your experiences change with time of night, location, and the associated characteristics of the sounds.

TETON HEARTLAND

Susan Chernak McElroy

The otter swam across the television screen and into my identity. "When I get out of school, I am going to work at Teton Marsh." I declared these words to my mother when I was six years old. I had just finished watching a Walt Disney program about an otter in the Grand Tetons. My mother responded, "That's nice, Dear." The incident was promptly forgotten and my dreams lay quiescent for twelve years.

When I was eighteen, a girlfriend asked what I was going to do when I graduated from high school later that year. With no direction from my conscious mind, my mouth opened and well-slept words came tumbling out: "I am going to work at Teton Marsh." My friend opened her plastic blue folder, pulled out a job application for Grand Teton National Park, and said, "I want to work in Yellowstone, but my folks sent me this application for Teton. Do you want it?" I asked, flabbergasted, "Where is Grand Teton National Park?"

On May 15th, just a few months later, I boarded my first plane to the Rockies. To take a job in Teton Park, I had completed my finals early and passed up senior cut day, my graduation, and the prom. A much more important, otter-induced celebration awaited me.

My first view of the Teton Mountains was from the airport runway. They were blue in the afternoon shadows, rising straight up out of the valley floor, without front running foothills to soften the distance from them to me.

A shuttle bus driver took me to the lodge where I would work as a cafeteria cook. Upon the way I eagerly asked him for directions to Teton Marsh. He knew of no such place. No one does. The location is fictional, although I did find many beaver- and bird-studded marshes, and ate a sandwich along the Snake River where the young Disney otter lost his family in a rock slide. I would come to know and love fiercely the green willow flats where the moose stood like great chocolate statues, and the breathtaking touch of rose on the mountain tops that splashed there just as I was walking to work each morning.

For the next seven years, I bounced back and forth from California to Jackson Hole, Wyoming, drawn back to that Rocky Mountain landscape against all reason. There was not enough steady work to keep even a small roof over my head and gas in my car. The Park and the town of Jackson shut down like a bear each fall. But there were coyotes trotting on the white frozen surface of Oxbow Bend, and eagles standing meditatively on the gut piles of elk carcasses after the hunting season. There was a silence in those mountains that was like the silence rising up from my belly in the middle of a long, restless night. There was a curve to the sage-studded hills that was like the curve of my own hip, and a color to the aspen bark that exactly mimicked my hair. The air was thin and heady and fresh as the twenty-something I was then, and the waters spoke in the same timbre as my own rushing voice. I wrote home to friends and family in a hopeless effort to describe the deep and precious melding I felt with this place: "If my body were a landscape, it would be this one."

There came a day when the voice of human culture called more loudly to me than the voice of the Teton Mountains, and I moved away, back to "real life" and a "real job" as an editor. But those particular craggy mountains would not let me leave the dance so easily. Having called to me since my childhood, they kept beckoning, harshly and ceaselessly.

Each week or two for the next twenty-five years, I dreamed of wandering in the town of Jackson, searching for work and an affordable apartment. My chest nearly melted in the presence of the dream mountains, and my heart neared breaking point. Many nights the memories and longings would awaken me to tears and sobs. In all those dreams, never once could I find my way back.

I told my rational mind that the Tetons must merely be a symbol for something else I was not finding in my life. The dreams could not possibly mean simply that I needed to move back to them. That was too easy, yet seemingly impossible from a practical point of view. But, twenty-five years later when I returned there as an author—a career that finally enabled me to keep a roof over my head in such a rural place—the dreams ceased and never returned. Not once.

And so I reflect deeply and humbly and constantly on the notion of siren landscapes, places that want us and will keep courting our souls until we take them as our mates, or die lonely someday without them. There are more luscious places I have lived in my life. Lands that were less harsh in winter, less windswept and aching in summer. Places with communities that are less suspicious, where good work can be found, and numbers of like-hearted, nature-reverent people abound.

I have finally surrendered to the insistent beckoning of this place. It is home now and ever, with its blasting winds, frigid winters, muddy springs, fragile-legged birds, tender foxes, and ghastly economics. It cannot escape me that I am rooted in a place where the elk I adore are hunted, where the coyotes that enchant me are shot like clay pigeons for fun, where the line between "tree-hugger" and "rancher" or "conservationist" and "wise-use proponent" is drawn in the sand with the blood of innocent creatures, tainted waters, and bulldozed soils. This is a place where my neighbor tells me that ground squirrels must be poisoned because they are "not good for Nature."

It would be my preference to hide from these heart-breaking assaults on this land that is so much a part of me, to live where I did not know first hand how many mountain lions were tracked down and killed for sport this season, or how high the *e-coli* count has risen in the river. Thich Nhat Hanh says that the most important thing we can do now is to hear the sound of Earth crying. If I were separated—my

20

soul living distant from this land that is my geographical body—perhaps that cry would be muffled. Living here, soul and body united in my own HeartLand, I hear the weeping in my bones, and it keeps me awake and alive.

The mountains have taught me that there is a landscape inside each person, calling to them, and that by harkening to this call, no matter what the cost of following this beseeching whisper, we are made bigger in our lives. Our work assumes a great integrity. Our growth in soul and spirit is co-facilitated by this precious land. Our challenges come up close and personal to dance and tussle with us, because we have the strength—the HeartLand within and surrounding us—to undertake a greater work.

"We can never go home again." According to whom? In truth, there is no place else *to* go.

Susan Chernak McElroy is a New York Times bestselling author, storyteller, and teacher. She has written numerous books, including the bestselling, *Animals as Teachers and Healers*, and has been featured in a host of anthologies that explore the connection between humans, animals, and the wild. Susan offers lectures and workshops on cultivating deeper appreciation for the wild within and without. She now resides in Bloomington, Indiana. Her website is http://www.susanchernakmcelroy.com.

PRACTICE:
EXPLORING THE HUMAN LANDSCAPE

- Find a time and place to sit quietly and undisturbed for at least a half-hour. Bring a writing pen, colored art pens or crayons, and a journal for recording observations.
- Practice "*Connecting with Nature*," page 55.
- Explore the following questions and activities:
  - If your body was a landscape, what kind of landscape would it be? What are the characteristics of this landscape? Draw a picture(s) of this human-landscape in your journal.
  - What kind of human activities are taking place in this landscape-of-you and what are the consequences? How might you change any of these activities that are having harsh "environmental" impacts?
  - Write a poem, song, or story about these activities and their transformation.
  - Has a landscape ever called to your soul by frequenting your thoughts, travel plans, choice of living location, etc.? If so, what are the characteristics of this landscape and how did you respond? What response(s) would be appropriate at this time?
- Write a love letter to this landscape, being sure to thank it for all that it has nourished within you.

WEATHERING THE STORM

Randy Smith

Storms! Loud, violent, fast, and torrential. Storms seemed to consume my short, but lightening years of youth.

I was a child born of the deep, lush, damp Adirondack Mountains, and as I grew, I trekked the forests like a ghost of James Fennimore Cooper's creation, sleeping under the canopy of stars and searching out my meals like all the other wild residents. Perhaps I was a strange boy. While so many of my peers played sports, acted in theater, and dedicated their weekends to family, friends, parties, or jobs, I bolted for tall timbers, climbing high to a wind swept perch and into my own imagination

No place charged my spirit more than a hidden, remote rocky mountaintop overlooking the Sacanadaga and Kunja-muck River Valleys, in the heart of the Adirondacks, a public forest preserve that had been protected for more than a century. My perch offered free admittance to gaze upon Nature's beauty and, at times, her frightening power and fury. When the storms weren't raging, this was a quiet, seemingly isolated place, absent of names and markers, with no trails leading to it, or noted in reference points on any map.

When the thunderstorms came, they rolled stealthily in, crept low under the skyline, pounced onto a valley, and slammed the mountainsides with all the intensity of hell on Earth. Man's firestorms are meek in comparison; these awesome displays of Mother Nature's raw energy reaffirmed her ability to give life and take it away despite, and perhaps in spite of, humanity's arrogance.

I would spend hours, even days, sitting upon the rocky skyline, imagining Mohawk warriors working up the valley below, or simply observing the infinite details of life's activities around me, none of which were man's doing. I knew intimately the birds and game that shared this loft and I often slept in their company under an old worn pine who had no bright green needles or youthful spring in his limbs or soft bark. He stood alone, living in this most exposed and harsh setting, scarred, knotted, and wounded by many a passing storm.

My first Adirondack storm came upon me when I still a free-spirited, skinny kid. It was a Saturday, in the fall. Free of chores and homework, I had rushed the afternoon's light to the mountaintop and disappeared into a headdress of clouds. Just as I approached the summit, a sharp, daring wind funneled in from neighboring peaks. It was a wind very different than any I'd known before. Deep rumbling, yet in the distance, foretold of what was to come. But I, naive as a newborn, nestled deep within the gigantic roots of that old pine. There, feeling secure, I waited and watched for the blackening skyline to tell its tale. Little did I know, I'd be witnessing the form and essence of my own life story.

Tiny droplets rained against my face. The sky darkened into shades of night. And, then, accompanied by a simultaneous explosion of lightening and thunder, harsh winds blasted me with torrents of ice-cold water. I had become the rocky shoreline against which an angry ocean breaks. I felt fear, pure fear. I trembled. I wept. I clung to the roots of that old tree as a terrified child does to a parent. I had never experienced such power, such unstoppable force, such undomesticated energy. This was Nature at her most horrifying, and, yet, deep within me I felt a sense of profound nurturing. I was cradled in awe, respect, and belonging.

Perhaps it was the baptismal effect of the rain or some sort of exorcism of humanity-imposed beliefs, but as I emerged from those roots, I felt reborn. I had been birthed into a new perception of the world. The late day sun revealed a mountaintop also renewed, bright and alive, re-quickened. I had weathered the storm and awakened, converted to the faith of Nature. The future seemed bright. Confident in Nature's love and my place within the natural world, I ventured home.

* * *

But, there is the world called "real" that yells out and demands that we make our way, even in our budding youth, through man-made trials and tests, and over hurdles measured and determined by so many others, all claiming qualification.

Swept away in the torrents of life far from home and familiar mountains, I found myself in uniform standing in strange lands, violent lands, filled with storms deadly and dangerous. There were no cool mountain breezes or quiet hidden sanctuaries. There was no rhythm to these storms, no method or reasoning, or any re-quickening, rejuvenating qualities. There was only the dry, burning desert winds choked with sand, rotten with the stench of man at his absolute worst, under the searing heat of an unchecked sun. Surrounded by so many men with empty, lonely feelings, I searched the distant skylines–everyday–for even a single pine, and found none.

My thoughts trekked into a place of inner solitude, into memories of that hidden cliff and senior pine. I wondered if that old weather-worn tree remembered me and waited for my return, my company, and my confessions. I wondered if the lightening of so many storms had finally broken those hardened knots of character that held it proudly, defiantly in the mountain sky. Or, perhaps, my growing depression ventured, I was just a fleeting moment in the hundreds of seasons that old pine endured. I might be forgotten, like the single snowflake that melts in mass at the end of an Adirondack winter.

Thrust into the real world, I did what was demanded for survival without thought or feeling. I buried what was most sacred and precious so very deep, hidden far inside an ever-charring heart. I grasped to remember the trails, the passageway, back to that place of rhythmic reason and cyclical order. Under stars, I prayed to make it back, even if to die, atop that windswept rocky peak in the safe embrace of the rugged pine. Death, on so many levels, came easy in the desert, but I feared meeting it amongst strangers, in strange lands. I did not want to spend eternity trying to get back to a resting place under that tree.

Months turned to years as my heart burned out and my spirit anguished. I fulfilled my duties as I was told and finally returned home to welcoming handshakes from old fat men who slapped my back and asked for details of a world they would never want to know.

In time my flesh and bones healed. They mended into twisted knots of scar tissue, bearing outwardly, forever, the storms I endured. In the mirror, I could count the trial lines etched in my face, on hard-thickened skin across a heavy brow of burdens that had layered upon me ever since the passing of youth. I forgot about my first life, what it was to be alive, and pressed on to measured successes in a rationally structured world; college, jobs, mortgages, new places, and new friends. I had all the trappings of a shining TV life; the good, bad, and ugly were all represented in full color.

That was the outside. Inwardly, I still found myself in conflicts in desolate places. I fortified myself against harsh realities and truths. I agonized, longing to quell the storms raging inside.

* * *

I was blessed with a daughter, bright, filled with energy, and possessing a strangely familiar fascination with Nature.

We explored the world, hand in hand, and we both grew. So many of the wonders of my youth came, slowly at first, like baby steps, to visit me once again. With each adventure, we wandered further and further into the forest and mountains, and into the places, sacred and precious, within me. We found secret retreats and refuges, meeting new and old residents in this land, it turned out, I had not forgotten. I reawakened to smells and flavors, as if layer upon layer of residue and scars from years of exposure to an artificial world of firepower were being surgically peeled away. I began to feel and sense, slowly at first, the human being buried as little more than ashes so long ago.

Under the banner of Thanksgiving and a visit to grandparents in the Adirondacks, we ventured deeper than ever before. Wandering, we found ourselves drawn far beyond the normal, reasonable range of an easy and safe Saturday afternoon hike. Winding along the river, on an old Mohawk trail, my daughter and I came to a place with no sign other than a haunting familiarity. And, as if ghosts within us had suddenly found their way, our physical selves were pulled from the trail.

We worked through the dense overgrowth. At times, I carried her on my back to speed the trek upward. For a child so young, she was surprisingly calm and quiet. Perhaps, I thought, she sensed something from me, between us.

I knew where we were going. Seemingly involuntarily, I pushed harder, racing an internal clock, as well as a darkening sky and the man-made watch on my wrist. I was headed there with both fear and childish excitement, and not understanding either. Boulders, terrain features, and odors all began to flood back at me from nightmarish years and dreams.

My chest screamed for oxygen and my forehead pounded as the blood rushed to keep me on my feet. We stopped only occasionally to share a juice box and answer the "Daddy, what's that?" questions.

The sky darkened. Common sense told me to turn around, to get myself and, more importantly, my little girl back to what was termed "safety." In my mind's ear, I could hear her mother panicking, raging at my neglect and decision to push on. All the voices of all the years in the "real" world bellowed and tore at me to turn around, to abandon this quest. We fought our way higher up the steep slope.

We began to crest the mountaintop just as the roar of an approaching thunderstorm echoed throughout the mountains. We slowed to small, soft, short steps, like those used when entering church. Through all my senses, I knew this place and its sacredness. We were here. After all those years, I was standing atop that rocky cliff, and I was holding my little girl's hand.

For a long time we stood there in silence. I don't know for how long. It was the question, "Daddy, what's wrong?" that brought me back to wipe a tear from my face. I don't think my daughter had ever seen me cry, and she was visibly concerned.

We stepped forward, me relying on her tiny hand to find the strength to walk. Amongst a pile of shattered limbs and scattered bark were the remnants of a once mighty and majestic pine, now a twisted, scarred, overgrown stump with massive roots grasping the rock face. I welcomed and found myself in awe of its still strong defiance, its ability to hold on for one last moment, one last visit.

We cleared a small space within the ball of gigantic roots that nearly consumed us, and sat there together, she on my lap, wrapped in the roots of my old friend. We talked about the tree, its life, and the hundred or more seasons it had witnessed over this valley and all who claimed it home. As lightening broke and thunder clapped around the neighboring mountains, my little girl flinched and clung tight to me. Nestled under my arms, her little fingers rubbed across and soothed those old scars and soul wounds.

My desert visions were true; I had come here to die. In that moment, I died to hardened ways of being and was gently born yet again into the authentic self that had been planted upon this ridge so long ago. I understood what that old weathered pine had taught me. I recalled what it meant to be safe, loved, and loving.

We watched the world unfold a true and real Adirondack thunderstorm. I did not flinch. A familiar sense of knowing filled me as I sat there in comfort, atop the mountain, understanding the storms I'd weathered. I was home.

Randy Smith lives in Baker City, Oregon with his wife, Mary, and daughter, Roarinbrook. He is the Interpretive Coordinator for eastern Oregon's state parks, and serves on a variety of committees, boards, and projects throughout the agency and his community. Before moving to Oregon from New York's Hudson Valley nearly three years ago, he worked in the nature and heritage education fields in New York state, as well as in the New York State park system. He has also owned his own executive security (bodyguard) business in the metro New York area, and, for many years, served with distinction as an airborne soldier in the U.S. Army, including several years of special operations tours overseas. He holds undergraduate degrees in environmental sciences and history, and completed graduate studies in public history at the State University of New York at Albany. Randy can be reached at: 3870 Indiana Ave., Baker City, OR 97814, USA; Randy.Smith@state.or.us.

PRACTICE:
LIVING NATURE AS METAPHOR

- Find a quiet place out-of-doors to work uninterrupted for at least an hour. Bring a writing pen, colored pens or crayons, and a journal for recording observations.

Part One

- Practice "*Connecting with Nature*" page 55, or engage in any other practice that will enable you to relax and become focused.
- Make a list of adjectives (e.g., stormy) that describe the patterns and trends in your life. Note: You can explore your entire life story, periods of specific time, or the current moment.
- Make a list of aspects of the natural world (e.g., storms) that are related to these adjectives.
- Collect adjectives together that are associated with certain natural phenomena and/or natural objects. (e.g., storms might be associated with dark, tumultuous, lightening fast insights, chaos, etc.)
- Review the role that these natural phenomena and/or natural objects have played in your life. In particular, explore their relationships to major life transitions and moments of deeper awakening—to your unique gifts, for example. What patterns do you notice?
- Write a poem, song, or story about these aspects of Nature and how they relate to your internal nature.

Part Two

- Identify a natural process that inspires you. Perhaps it is the metamorphosis of a caterpillar into a butterfly, or the blossoming of a flower, or the way trees can bend and brace in a magnificent storm.

- Make a list of steps and/or adjectives that characterize this process.
- Draw one or more pictures that illustrate the process.
- Consider this natural process as a metaphor for your future. What emotions does it bring up? What does it inspire you to do? How does it inspire you to act with regard to other people, the environment, and your own needs?
- Write a poem, song, or story about your future, incorporating this life metaphor.
- Place the pictures, list of adjectives, and what else you wrote where you can see them regularly.
- Repeat this process anytime you are feeling stuck or want to be even more inspired to live your life fully.

NATIVES, GHOSTS, TRANSPLANTS

K. Lauren de Boer

My love for the land between two rivers simmered slowly for years. It would only become a well-flavored broth when I had learned to become enamored with ghosts and transplants, to make the loss of the dispossessed my own, and to accept the strident claims of the present. This land named Iowa—an expanse stretching between the Mississippi River to the east and the Missouri river to the west—was once riotous with diverse life. Hard maples and bur oaks dominated the river bluffs. Woodland ravines wore cloaks of beautiful ferns, interspersed with diverse softwoods and forest wildflowers like yellow ladies-slippers, jack-in-the-pulpit, and trout lily.

But Iowa was to become the most deeply altered terrain on the North American continent. By 1900 two thirds of the 6.7 million acres of forest cover in Iowa—gorgeous stands of white oak, red cedar, and hard maple—had disappeared; 3,000 miles of rivers had been dammed and channelized; vast wetlands were drained out of existence. In slightly less than one human life span, a 30-million-acre blanket of tallgrass prairie was reduced to one tenth of one per cent of its former size—a mere 30,000 acres—by the plow. The names are legion: Bluestem, dropseed, compass plant, coneflower, gentian, and blazing star. Successive waves of transformation—pioneer settlement, agriculture, gypsum and coal mining, the railroad, the creation of giant recreational reservoirs—swept through. Vast communities of prairie grasses and wildflowers became huge tracts of non-native grassland or mono-cultured farmland. Frost aster, switchgrass, phlox, prairie anemone, hoary vervain, coreopsis were given their untimely leave. And, with this habitat gone, abundant populations of elk, bison, wild turkey, deer, prairie chickens, bear, wolves, river otter, beaver, waterfowl, and shorebirds vanished. White wild indigo, june grass, purple meadow rue, sawtooth sunflower, Scribner's panic grass…and more than 200 additional prairie plants.

As a young man in a small town in the heart of the state, something in this ravaged landscape won my heart. It began with a trip one summer day to an isolated rural spot on the Des Moines River.

* * *

To reach the Des Moines river valley, I drive due south from Prairie City past white, two-storied clapboard farm-houses, A-frame pig sties, silos, tiny country churches, and patchwork fields of sorghum, soybeans, and corn. The road follows the contour of long rolling hills blanketed with some of the richest soil on Earth, formed from a departed sea of tallgrass prairie. Redwing blackbirds, brown-headed cow-birds, and English house sparrows dominate the farmyards and fence posts.

Just when I feel that this roadscape will roll on with-out end, I pass over the rise of a hill and abruptly hit gravel. The fields go wild and brambly and I osmos, as if through a membrane, into another realm. The old Rambler station wagon rumbles and clunks over the roadbed. Dust roils up and anoints everything in a kind of strange baptism. I grind it in my teeth and my hair turns bristly. The road is now little more than a dirt path. The purr of the 6-cylinder engine and the rattle of the springs accompany the drone of cicadas in roadside transplants: Ragweed, Queen Anne's lace, and now feral hemp planted in World War II as fiber for rope produc-tion. When I reach an abandoned gypsum mine now filled from periodic floodwaters and an underground spring, I stop and get out. I hunker down in the weeds on its banks and peer into the water. Bass, bluegill, and green sunfish hang in the crystal water as if on a string, turning slowly to meet my shadow. They glide and stop. Glide and stop. The stop is sudden and perfect, like blinking out a frame of the action. It is high summer and so the carp have surfaced in raucous schools, their soft mouths extended to suck the surface. An Asian fish, I realize. More transplants, making their way, eating the eggs of natives. I toss a pebble and their scattering boils the water with a golden flash of scales.

I head across some rusted rail tracks, then down through a labyrinth of summer plant growth, emerging suddenly on the bank where the river does an almost hairpin turn. The flow is very deep here, so deep the river appears oddly still, even though I know the current is moving across the river-bed with sure steady strength. I imagine the murky world down there, picturing the giant bottom-dwellers I'd seen in the backs of pick-ups and in photographs in the Outdoor section of the Des Moines Register. These catfish hung, big as a small man, on stout poles between two people. It was said they came from a hidden place on the river, a well-kept secret from anyone but the locals. That place, my brother's father-in-law finally revealed to me, was this turn in the river where I stand. Years ago, a train had derailed here and the boxcars that tumbled into the river were left to the elements. "They spawn in those cars," was his only elaboration on his revelation.

I pick my way across logs and rocks out to a perch on a rusty boxcar protruding above water. Feeling the dust and heat from the drive, I rashly plunge in. The current is swifter than I anticipate and before I'm able to reach the far bank, I'm swept downstream to a long strip of sand. I go to explore the trees lining the beach; but as I near them, I see that they are only the ghosts of trees, the shells of giant drowned bur oaks, gray, stark, and weathered against the sky. Their brittle branches are adorned with long ivies, the barkless trunks cloaked with brilliant green mosses. Blue herons retreat in lazy, lumbering flight on my approach. The dried mud crack-ling beneath my bare feet bears no footprints, only the tracks of receding floodwaters. This strange forest, with its unlikely beauty, was wrought from an Army Corps of Engineers proj-ect to create the Red Rock recreational reservoir in 1969.

* * *

Years later, in the fall of the year, I return, perhaps to fish, perhaps just to turn rocks at the edge of the water. This time the drive to the river passes the Neil Smith National Wildlife Refuge, a newly established 5,000-acre preserve dedicated to restoring tallgrass prairie and savanna habitat.

A crisp October day turns by slow increments into a delicious suspension in time. I catch no fish, so I idly watch the sky as an endless, shifting, cavorting crowd twists and turns in strands and dots against ochre-lit clouds. The migrating waterfowl pass for hours overhead. Their calls and wing beats move lucidly in and out of my consciousness, like thoughts and images in those fragile moments between sleep and waking. Something jars loose in me and runs untethered with the river. In its steady flow, I feel the tug, the relentless claim nature holds on all things, indifferent to possessor or dispossessed. An unaccountable beauty extends out of the mundane and the lost, shining out of the gray silence of bur oaks. I study the boxcars and discover that these intruders, too, have become an intricate part of the form of this place. I slowly realize that I am surrounded by my own kind. There is something in me of all of them - the transplants, migrants, and ghosts; the opportunists, the natives, and the dispossessed.

A pheasant, too near, crows loudly, startling me out of my reverie—yet another transplant. I take this as a sign and head for home. Out of this wounded land—a river valley once nestled by prairie and shaded by forest—the steady sure pulse of life continues to combine, configure, adjust, and restore. A fragile beauty simmers, its strange and gathering flavors waiting to be tasted.

K. Lauren de Boer was the Executive Editor of *EarthLight, Journal for Ecology and Spirituality* (www.earthlight.org) from 1995-2006. His interviews, essays, and poetry have been published and reprinted in several publications and an-thologies and he has interviewed dozens of leading edge vi-sionaries and thinkers in the area of ecology, spirituality, and consciousness. In 2008, he published a collection of poetry, *Where It Comes From.* Lauren has taught a course on Sus-tainability and Culture at Naropa University and is currently the core faculty member for the Institute for Educational Studies / Endicott College in the Masters of Education in Integrative Learning and the Great Work. Lauren currently serves on the board for the Institute for Sacred Cinema and is on the advisory board for the Center for Ecozoic Studies in Greensboro, North Carolina. Lauren can be reached at: 111 Fairmount Ave., Oakland, CA 94611, USA; klauren@ earthlight.org.

38

PRACTICE:
EXPLORING THE HUMAN LANDSCAPE

- Dress appropriately for the weather so that you can remain comfortable in the out-of-doors for at least an hour. Bring an adequate supply of water, a cushion or chair to sit on and a compass if you so choose, and a pen and journal for recording your observations.
- Go to a safe place out-of-doors. This place might be very near your home or quite remote.
- Practice "*Connecting with Nature*" page 55.
- Sit down facing North, close your eyes, and allow your thoughts to become still (give yourself at least a few minutes to calm your mind).
- Open your eyes and allow them to softly focus on some aspect of the landscape in front of you—perhaps it is a tree, a bird, a stone, or a mountain.
- Ask yourself, "If this aspect of nature was a mirror, what would it be reflecting back to me about myself?"
- Notice what comes into your awareness—perhaps it is aspects of your character that it is time for you to let go of or transform, or aspects of your life that warrant celebration and gratitude, or a deeper awakening to your unique gifts. Journal your observation.
- Repeat the question, observations, and journaling while facing East, then South, then West.
- Make an offering of gratitude to the place (perhaps each direction while reciting what you learned). The offering might be comprised of water, prayer ties (see page 132), a poem, song, etc.
- Repeat the entire process routinely in the same and different locations. Notice if any patterns emerge with respect to the aspects of nature that serve as a mirror or in reference to each of the directions.

WHERE THE LOST ARE FOUND

Jason Kirkey

I awoke to a world cloaked white with snow, and Nature's promise that school would be cancelled for the day. We were in the midst of a blizzard; already the snow looked to be half a foot deep. Those of us who have been raised in "western culture" have been conditioned to find value in tangible things. Yet, in those moments of waking, I found myself amazed at the beauty arising out of the stark, colorless world. Something beckoned me to step out into the frozen day, to search for beauty in the emptiness of my own form.

I was thirteen, and like most people of that age, had experienced no world other than the one I was raised in. There was school and homework, chores, junk food. I killed time with friends in front of the television and video games, and with other entertainment addictions. My life was arranged around escaping from the daily mundane and entering a realm of life-suspending numbness. On most days, I hadn't a care in the world.

But there were other days. Days marked by a profound sense of sadness, and a permeating emptiness. I felt deracinated in my teens; as if I had some how been uprooted, torn away, from a life-defining sense of place and Spirit. And while many in today's world would say I was merely a typical teenager, some part of me, deep within, knew that there was more to life and living.

My home was archetypal America—placed in a small suburban town, denoted and delineated by concrete. There were very few natural places left. As a boy I was often bereft of aimless wandering and adventures in the "great outdoors." Little wild-life survived. I felt lost, disconnected, alienated from both wild Nature and my wild soul.

I had always had an affinity for the natural world,

but I had viewed it the only way I knew how—as a curious observer, like someone watching the snow fall on the other side of the window, longing to go outside yet unable to find the door. I acted as most of our society does; as if I were entirely independent of my environment. There was me and there was everything else.

My young life felt stale and unanimated. Yet, some aspect of me said that opening myself up to Nature might reenliven my world, and bring me into contact with something yet unknown and special. So, on this day, I was determined to go out into the world, the *real* world of Nature, to find that something. I had a sense that a fundamental piece of my self was missing, and that it lay in waiting, just at the edge of the forest.

My restlessness and longing were stirred by questions and a cousin. I had openly been questioning my belief in the transcendent God of Christianity and studying druidic traditions for about a year. The Druids believe that Nature is sacred and that divinity is to be found in and around all beings. It was the words of my cousin, which had first opened me to the possibility of this new, yet old way of perceiving. He had asked me to look out the window at the trees. "Nature," he said, "does not require us to believe in it; it is right here for us to experience."

And so I went in search, hoping to find what was out there; and perhaps *in here*.

Two friends and I arrived at the forest. It was flaked in utter silence.

For years, these woods had been a place for teenagers and lost souls to drink and party. Beer cans, gasoline containers, old and broken bikes, and other assorted hallmarks of a throw away society lay buried in the snow. But I knew little of the wasteland aspects of this place at that time. It was my first visit there, and to me it seemed holy.

I could sense eyes on me, and yet knew my friends had wandered some distance away. I felt exposed, seen, and confused. Was I the watched or the watcher? Spirits, the Druids believe, tend toward wild places, and this forest was haunted. Any city or town that starts absent-mindedly paving over Nature serves an eviction notice to the spirits of the place, the *anima loci*. And so, like myself, I believe, they had come here in exile, hoping to once again set their roots, to become grounded. After only moments in the *real* world, it was becoming less clear where I ended and Nature began.

I settled down next to an old oak tree in the heart of the small forest. It reached upward in twists and spirals. I imagined it cradling the heavens in its branches, while hugging Earth in its roots. The Celtic people, and their shaman-like Druids, considered trees sacred, and each tribe had as their center an oak, yew, or ash, which served as their world tree; a doorway between this world and the numinous Otherworld. Oaks in particular were considered by some tribes to be the "king of the forest." The Old Irish word for the oak is *duir*, and is related to the Sanskrit root that gives us the English word "door."

I shivered from both the chill and fear. Perhaps it was fear of the unknown, or an intimation of what Mircea Eliade calls the *mysterium tremendum*, the feeling of awe and terror in the experience of the sacred. I swallowed my fear and slowly approached the oak, resting my ungloved hand upon its trunk. Its bark was rough and cold, but I thought I could feel a pulse of life, as if an inner warmth enlivened it.

Unconsciously, I began to speak to the tree. Silent words formed and were uttered within my head. My conscious mind, taken by surprise, reminded me that oaks don't speak English. And yet I continued introducing myself, telling it who I was and why I was here. I told it I was just a young kid, feeling lost and adrift in a world that made no sense to me. I unburdened myself to it and prayed that it might have some wisdom to pass on to me; guidance toward a way to live my life in participation with Nature and the sacred. I wanted to claim that piece of my life that seemed to be missing.

To my surprise the tree answered back. Or, my now nervous ego proposed, was I just making up an answer in my head? Is it more mad to speak with a tree or to speak for a tree?

The tree seemed alive and awake beneath my hand, as if an effervescent spirit radiated from within. There was an awareness to this tree that made it seem not so much an object, but a presence. I recognized the voice as my own, but its source came from a deeper place, where my hand met the rough of the bark. Somehow the oak and I had communicated, and I had understood in my own way what the tree had "said."

The tree's message to me was clear. It was not so much something I saw or heard that delivered the message, but rather a feeling of belonging in the presence of this being. A long lost part of myself suddenly animated and vitalized. I knew then that I am a part of Nature, not apart from it, no matter how close the concrete and distant the forest. The separation of my soul from the tree's soul is only an illusion. So it is with all beings; humans, animals, rocks, mountains, oceans, and rivers. We are all woven of the same spirit.

My friends returned from their own explorations, and we packed up to go home.

Yet, I had come home. I had come home within my body and within the greater community of Life. There was a longing in me to belong to the Earth, and I gave myself over to it. As I reached out to the tree, it somehow leaned back towards me, and the rest of the world with it. Where once I had felt emptiness, I was now filled with a sense of connectedness. I experienced the world as a web of relationships, which I was a part of.

How could I do anything but begin to act from that place? By engaging with the wildness of Nature, I was opened to the opportunity to inhabit the wilds of my soul, and the abandon to relate deeply with it, and thus to tune into the numinous quality of Life. And it became hard to find the mundane in the days and nights of a thirteen year old boy.

I returned often to the woods, establishing a relationship with the beings there, feeling a kinship and belonging to that tiny patch of land that succeeded in coaxing out my still-wild soul. I came to see that great oak as an elder of the forest, and a good friend.

I cleaned the woods of garbage, and on a few occasions stopped teenagers from starting fires. This feeling of stewardship, of caretaking the land, grew in me, and I came to understand my responsibility to Earth as a whole. It engendered within me a sense of worldly belonging and reciprocity.

The woods were a forest shrine to me, what the Irish call a *fidnemed*. That small forest was the place that opened my soul to the spirit of Nature, guiding me into the druidic Otherworld. It was the place where I first felt a true sense of kinship with the other-than-human.

Nature is always a place where the lost can be found.

Jason Kirkey grew up in Massachusetts. He is a poet, a student of mindfulness practice, and practitioner of a blend of Buddhist and earth-centered Irish spirituality. He holds an Interdisciplinary degree from Naropa University in Boulder, Colorado with concentrations in Environmental Studies and Contemplative Psychology. In 2006 he founded Hiraeth Press and is the author of three collections of poetry, *Portraits of Beauty*, *Songs from a Wild Place*, and *The Ballad of the Sea-Sweet Moon and Other Poems*. His website is www.jasonkirkey.com.

PRACTICE:
STORYTELLING WITH THE SPIRITS OF PLACE

- Dress appropriately for the weather and the length of time that you wish to spend out-of-doors (at least an hour recommended).
- Bring a pen and journal, adequate supply of water, and cushion or chair to sit on if you choose.
- Locate a natural place that feels special to you—or that calls to you. This might be a wilderness area, your back-yard, or even a small urban garden.
- Consciously step into the spiritscape of the land by let-ting go of your mental "focus" on the forms around you and inviting your body to sense the essence of what is there. Tune into sensations in your physical body, as well as your emotions.
- Recommendation: Practice *"Connecting with Nature"* page 55.
- Introduce yourself to the place, sharing something of your intent for being there.
- Invite a spirit of the place to introduce itself to you. Once you have a sense that you have been spoken to (pay at-tention to the feelings in your "gut"), envision this tree, rock, animal, etc. as an ensouled being and sit beside it.
- Ask the spirit of the place to tell you its story.
- Listen with the ears of your heart.
- Ask yourself what that story has to teach you about your own life journey. Journal your observations.
- Ask the spirit of the place what it would like in reciproc-ity for its story—some water, a song, prayer ties (see page 132), or perhaps the telling of your own story. Make the offering with gratitude and continue upon your path.
- Repeat this practice often, observing synchronicities and increases in your intuitive abilities.

PRACTICE:
ENVIRONMENTAL CLEAN UP

Part One

- Formally (e.g., through an "adopt a street or beach or park etc." program) or informally choose a natural location near your home where you can practice land stewardship.
- Visit this location routinely (at least once a month, perhaps on the full moon) and remove any waste that has been dumped there.
- Note any violations (e.g., dumping, vandalism, poaching) and report them to the appropriate authorities.
- If you own the land or have permission from the landowners, enhance the property for wildlife by adding native plants and boxes for native wildlife, such birds, bats, and bees.

Part Two

- Familiarize yourself with the "Nature as Mirror" practice (page 38) and apply it when you visit your environmental stewardship location by focusing on the human-alterations and impacts to the site. Note: Bring a pen and journal.
- What emotions arise? What memories? What beliefs about yourself, other people, and the land?
- What "garbage" do you need to clean up in your own life? What violations to your inner landscape need to be reported?
- Journal your observations.
- In what ways can you enhance the beauty and abundance of the landscape-of-you?
- Do so, and enjoy the results.

AT THE HEART OF ECSTASY

Jamie K. Reaser

Trailside shore of babbling brook.
Sunflecked glade of forested nook.
Young girl searches with innocent eyes,
Singing melody to the tune of Nature's sighs.
Gaining knowledge, sharing glee,
Earth's cradled daughter me.
Today a woman walking tall.
Forever a wisp of Nature's call.
(1990)

I've only had one truly intimate relationship in my life.
It was with a brook, and I was seven.

My family had moved from Roanoke, Virginia, to Bask-
ing Ridge, New Jersey. My role in the process was that
of protestor. I had absolutely no desire to experience the
"change that would be good for me" and I wasn't about to
be separated from my best friends—a cadre of golden-eyed
toads that lived, by virtue of their own missteps, in the window well beside the front door. I moped and threw excep-
tional temper tantrums. Finally, with less than an hour to
go before Bessie, our large white Buick station wagon, was
to head north, my wilted parents put a cardboard box in my
hand. I carefully extracted a few toads from the landscaping
trap, yanked wads of grass from the lawn and climbed into
the backseat with my all-too-compliant younger sisters.

Temperatures are colder in New Jersey than Virginia.
That was the first lesson I learned upon arrival at our new
home. It was fall, and back in Virginia the toads would have
at least another month before they needed to be released
from the window well for hibernation. Yet, the temperature
that late afternoon in New Jersey was scolding; one way or

another I was going to have to learn to let go of my attachment to the toads.

I carried the box to the edge of woods and placed each gorgeous amphibian upon the leafy ground. Worry and guilt intermingled with the grief of goodbye. Would they be able to find a place to hibernate quickly enough? Had my greedy need for their company doomed them? I rubbed my young fingers across their dry, warty backs. To this day, I still wonder about their fate.

The winter months passed without leaving any particular mark on my memory.

Spring returned and so did my health problems. I was a sickly child. By the time the trees were again leafing I was so weak from the latest illness that I could barely stand. A previous infection had caused brain damage and paralyzed my right side. According to the doctors, I would be forever challenged by "neurological impairment" and "poor motor coordination." Simply put, I was a foggy-minded klutz now frustratingly bound to bed and sofa. In my opinion there could have been little worse than being told to make do indoors with my sisters' doll house, Barbies, and Shawn Cassidy records.

Finally one summer morning my parents placed me in a lawn chair near the brook that ran behind our house. The chair was itself a site to behold; a light aluminum frame woven with pea soup green and neon orange-and-yellow strappings. My mother had been a home economics major and prided herself on her decorating skills. This chair and its counterparts had no doubt been expertly selected to illustrate the ideal 1970s porch decorum. It was quite uncomfortable.

In front of me a lavish patch of jewelweed stood erect with orange pendulant blooms open for business. Bees snuggled into the flower mouths and wriggled their bodies against the inner walls. When they backed out, they shimmered golden yellow pollen. After a brief hiatus, as if to catch their breath, they were off to the next flower. I was too young to be thinking about sex. But that's what I was watching: plant sex enabled by pimping bees.

I looked back over my shoulder to observe my parents subduing the weeds that would need at least a couple generations to take over the property. Weapons of domestication were hoisted into the air and then flung with force against thick and creeping greenery. From time to time a lawn mover roared, or a weed eater. It was during events such as this that I learned cuss words. My body can still recall the contrasting sense of serenity in front of me and frenetic chaos behind.

When was the first time you knew that you didn't fit in? This moment might not have been my first moment, but it was definitely such a moment. My mind pondered the deep upwellings of a frustrated, unhappy child. Wrong family? Wrong body? Wrong place and time? I turned my gaze again to Harrison Brook and the jewelweed at its banks.

He was buzzing inches from my face chattering in a high pitched staccato. His wings beat so fast and close I couldn't fully see them, and yet his body remained motionless—suspended. Two small black eyes met mine. The sun reflected off his iridescent feathers: head and back green, stomach white, throat crimson. A ruby-throated hummingbird.

I swear he pierced my heart.

Every aspect of my being gushed open. And either the entire landscape swelled into me or I expanded to encompass it. I'm really not sure what went in which direction. That bird, the flowers, the bees, the water, the water striders, the pollywogs, the minnows, the mayfly larvae and crayfish, the sandy shore up the other bank and forest and its hidden life beyond were, for an instant, formless. One energy throbbed, quickening in my heart—babumbabum babumbabum—in unison with the heart of Earth.

I could see, hear, and feel with a sensitivity that seemed to ravish my body. Everything of color was vibrant. What lacked color had depth. The brook sounds collected into an orchestra with deep water, surface water, cascading water, and fish-jumping-out-and-back-into-water instruments. The sun pursed its dry lips against my skin. In later years, I would learn the word ecstasy and define it by that moment.

The hummingbird moved on and with time, so did my illness. For the next five years I grew up in and alongside that brook. My feet learned to navigate algaed stones. My toes played games in oozing mud. I held soft, bulbous-bodied bullfrog tadpoles in the cup of my hands, and watched suckers swim in and out of the holes they made at the base of the clay banks. I caught water snakes and got bitten, frequently. Once I saw a pair of wood turtles mating under water. I sang songs to everything.

I busted leg-hold traps set for raccoons or muskrats. I refused to tell the neighborhood bullies where Tom, the large snapping turtle, hid or the whereabouts of the bronze-colored bullfrog that screamed like a child when taken in hand. Anyone who showed up with a fishing pole would get directed away from the one pool where rainbow trout still churned.

Eventually my sisters and I were packed up into another Buick station wagon, a blue one named Moby Dick, and driven away from Harrison Brook. It is unlikely that I cried that day, but would have had it been permitted.

Over the years, I learned more biology than I experienced. And I made sure that others knew the facts. By the time I was mid-way through college I had become a tall, skinny environmental activist-force to be reckoned with. It didn't matter whether it was the rainforests in trouble or the ozone layer or some animal getting stitched into a coat, I cared and I was damn well going to make sure people changed their ways. People were a problem. They were a threat to all that I loved.

In the summer of 1989 my environmental leadership activities had positioned me atop a horizontal timber three stories above the ground. People, too many of them in my opinion, were shouting from behind, below, and in front. "Keep going!" "Don't look down!" "Take the next step!"

I had climbed and scaled the ropes without hesitation. But now, mid-beam, I found myself inexplicitly frozen. Paralyzed. A male broad-tailed hummingbird whizzed up to my face, fluttered, chittered, looked me in the eye, and sped onward.

I broke into sobs.

I had forgotten.

That night I sat beside a campfire and a mountain stream encircled by my Outward Bound instructor and other Leadership America participants. With tears rolling down my face I told them about the ruby-throated hummingbird, Harrison Brook, and the intimate moments of my childhood. I told them what I had forgotten: When the heart is fully open, distinctions melt away. There is no us. No them. How could I have invited a deep connection with the natural world and yet excluded the human animal? Nature had never isolated me.

Under shooting stars and the spread wings of a great grey owl, to the sound of trout jumping for white moths above dark waters, I made a vow. I let go of the anti-human perspective of environmental conservation and claimed a new vision, one that sees "conservation" as an art and science of motivating and empowering people into a deep and enduring relationship with Nature. I vowed to invite people into my heart in the way I would invite a nestling song bird or a golden-eyed toad. I vowed to heal my own relationship with my own species, as well as foster *Homo sapiens'* re-connection with the land—the true and only root of our humanity. That night, people became a part of the landscape for me.

My life now is not so much different than that of a pimping bee. I move from person to person spreading tiny grains of consciousness in the hope of fertilizing what will gradually emerge, grow, blossom, and unfold into a beautiful relationship among humans and all other beings. This is no mere act of intercourse. It is my intent to make love. The kind of ecstatic love that pierces the human heart.

Jamie K. Reaser, Ph.D. believes in the potential of the human spirit. She is a practitioner and teacher of ecopsychology, nature-based spirituality, and various approaches to expanding human consciousness, as well as a conservation ecologist, wilderness rites-of-passage guide, poet, writer, artist, and homesteader-in-progress. She is the author or editor of more than 100 publications, including *Bring Back the Birds: What You Can Do to Save Threatened Species.* Her photographs, illustrations, and poems appear in books, magazines, and calendars. She makes her home at Ravens Ridge Farm, 85 magical acres in the Blue Ridge Mountains of Virginia. Jamie can be reached at Ravens Ridge Farm, 1207 Bull Yearling Road, Stanardsville, VA 22973, USA; ecos@nelsoncable.com. More information on her work can be found at: http://www.jamiekreaser.com.

PRACTICE:
CONNECTING WITH NATURE

Part One: Getting Grounded

- Dress appropriately to be out-of-doors for at least an hour.
- Bring an adequate supply of water, pen, and journal.
- Go to a place in nature that you will be safe and uninterrupted. This location might be just outside your home or school or in a remote wilderness setting.
- Choose a specific location and stand there with your head looking forward and your shoulders back and down slightly.
- Place your hands in prayer position at chest height
- Take a quick inward breath through your mouth as you tilt your hands toward your face, so that the finger tips end up pointing to your lower jaw.
- Repeat this in rapid sets of three. On the first breath set the intent to bring the breath to your belly button area, the second to your heart, and the third to the area between your eye brows.

Part Two: Becoming Centered

- Take in a long, deep breath.
- While holding the breath, turn your head to the left, then right, and bring it back to center.
- Release the breath at the center point.
- Repeat in sets of three. You can, as before, choose to breath into each of the three energy centers.

Part Three: Opening Your Heart

- Bring your hands into prayer position at chest height.
- Extend them, hands together, toward the ground and say "Earth."

- Extend them straight out in front of you, still held together, and say "Nature."
- Extend them straight above your head, held together, and say "Sky or Cosmos."
- Separating the hands, lower each to your sides, shoulder height and say "Balance."
- Bring them back to prayer position at chest height and them draw them together to the chest and say "Heart."
- Repeat in sets of three.

Part Four: Inviting In Nature's Energies

- Extend your right arm above your head as far as you can reach and wiggle the fingers on your right hand. See and feel (or at least imagine) the energies from the sun and other aspects of Nature coming into your hand. You might even cup your hand and imagine a handful of energy–golden–forming there.
- Extend your left arm above your head as far as you can reach.
- Bring your right hand to your left hand, and imagine spreading the energy into your left hand and down your arm.
- Bring both hands together to your heart and let the energy enter your body.
- Bring your hands to the ground and imagine releasing any lingering mental heaviness (e.g., anxiety, doubts, "to do list" distractions) there.
- Repeat in sets of three until you feel the flow and lightness of Nature moving through you.

Part Five: Introducing Yourself To Nature

- Lift up your shirt, exposing your belly button (Note: in some indigenous cultures the belly button is considered the door way to the soul).
- Place your right hand over your belly button and open it forward as if it were a door with the hinges at your

wrist.

- Walk around repeating this procedure while "saying hello" to aspects of nature (e.g., trees, the sky, the earth, bird). You might also want to try this with other people and "man-made" objects.
- Notice how you feel and what images or thoughts come to mind.

Variation: Lay face down upon the earth with your belly-button exposed. Breathe in and out as if through your belly button. Repeat several times.

If you so choose, journal your observations for each of these practices. You might also want to draw pictures or write poems or songs (etc.) that reflect your experience.

Credit: These practices are modifications of those taught to JKR by don Americo Yabar, a shaman and mystic of the Q'ero Nation in the Peruvian Andes.

A WALK IN A CHILD'S MIND

Ilene Zwerin

I was brought up in a loving home, in a time and place where there was no need for a key to the house. We lived in the Mohawk Valley, on the outskirts of Utica, New York, about a thirty-minute drive from the Adirondack Mountains—Mountains millions of years old, rounded and gentled by time. Mountains blessed with lakes and waterways and blanketed with an endless cover of deciduous and evergreen forests.

In 1894 this land was designated a state park, dotted with privately held parcels bought for a pittance by the wealthy who built great "camps." Although most of these parcels have been divided up and sold to others who in turn built smaller "camps," much of the Adirondacks remain undeveloped and roadless. The largest wild land preserve in the United States outside of Alaska, the Adirondacks can still foster a belief in paradise.

My parents first took me into the Adirondacks in 1954. I was seven years old and I felt like someone had just handed me the keys to the kingdom.

Our day started early one morning in June. My parents loaded me into the family car and drove north out of the Mohawk Valley, leaving my sister behind with my grandparents. I had come of age and there was a whole new world about to unfold before me.

In ten minutes we were climbing out of the valley and up Deerfield Hill. Looking out the rear window, I could see the gentle rolling farm hills and the ribbon of the Mohawk River. Next to the river were the train tracks that lead to New York City, three hundred miles away. It might as well have been three hundred light years.

In fifteen minutes, we were winding our way through

pine forests on a narrow mountain road. In an hour, we were turning down a small dirt road and driving under an archway that said "Eagle Cove." We pulled up in front of a cabin, where a man escorted us to some large wooden porch chairs. He had been waiting for us and knew my parents. I had never met him.

We sat there talking, mostly adult talk. How boring. I was far more interested in the birds and squirrels flitting about. As I sat there sipping hot cocoa, my feet not even touching the ground, I longed to be turned loose in this enchanted land.

Through the trees I could see a distant lake. Finding a moment of silence in the conversation, I asked if we could go down there. No doubt they sensed I was getting fidgety, but there was more talk yet to come. I was granted my freedom and told to follow the path down to the lake. There, I would find a boathouse and someone named Nancy.

When you are seven years old, even a small corner of the world seems a big place. I was off on a great adventure. I was to find my way alone through this strange forest, along a path I had never been on, and to a boathouse I had never before visited. Surely, I could find my way.

Walking down the path, I soon lost sight of the cabin and my parents, but the lake ahead seemed no closer. My heart was beating wildly. I was in no man's land—and I was by myself. I was in a thick forest with no fields or horses or gardens or familiar sounds of civilization. And the lake was barely visible, or was that just the sky? For the first time in my young life I was aware of nature untouched by humans. I had never felt so alive.

The moment of truth was before me. Should I turn back to the safety of what I knew or should I forge ahead into uncharted territory? The answer was clear. Forge ahead.

I don't know what made me step off the path. Maybe it was to get a better look at the squirrel that was chattering at me. I started walking on the soft forest floor and felt exhilarated. What would happen to me if I continued off the path? Could I find my way back?

I looked around to get my bearings. At first I looked for markers, natural signs, that could later help me return to the path. I became amazed; these markers were much more than just tools to help me keep to my course. Like the faces of my friends and family, each tree, each flower, and every rock had its own unique identity. Even the roll and texture of the forest floor had a character that changed with every step. I began to realize that everything around me was just as much a part of the world as I was.

I walked deeper and deeper into the woods in awe. I came to a stream and it told me it was on its way down to the lake. If I followed it I would end up on the lakeshore and could find the boathouse. The Earth was showing me the way. The Earth and all God's creations were speaking a language as understandable as my parent's voices, and far more interesting.

All of my senses were being used to their full potential for the first time. My eyes caught the slightest movement, and my ears the slightest sound. Even my skin was sending me messages. A slight breeze brought a scent that was unfamiliar. I stopped to better identify the smell and realized how much noise I had been making. I sat down and remained perfectly still, watching, listening, and sniffing the air.

Out of the corner of my eye I saw movement and a doe came into view. As small as I was, she looked huge. Casually, she went to the stream and started drinking. When the doe finally realized I was there, she raised her head, alert and curious. Looking into her soft brown eyes, I could feel her compassion. I wasn't any bigger than the fawn at her side and she seemed to know that I was as vulnerable. I had the distinct feeling that this four-legged creature could be my mother, just as easily as the woman back on the porch. I realized then that every mother's bond is the same with her child. I belonged to a family not limited by humanness.

I sat there quietly in the deer's presence until she moved off. Then I slowly followed the stream down to the lake, noticing trees, squirrels, insects, crayfish, soil, sky, and water as I went. Everything around me came in through my senses. My soul knew us to be equal in God's eyes. In those woods, I found an internal knowing beyond words.

In my child's heart a seed was planted from which I would grow forth. Nature would forever shape my life and hold the answers to my most important questions. The basis of existence is so simple—knowledge of the universe exists in everything.

As an adult, I have since returned to the woods by the lake. The man who owned the camp has passed away and so have my parents. Although acid rain has had a devastating effect on lakes in the Adirondacks, the land is still there, seemingly as pristine and beautiful as when I was a child. Retracing my steps, I was surprised to find that what seemed like an odyssey to a child was just a short walk in the woods for an adult. Nevertheless, the journey through the forest of my internal terrain had been one of epic proportions. I had learned to honor and respect all of creation. I am a part of everything.

Ilene Zwerin lives with husband, Mark, and her two dogs, Digger and Jiggs, in Jackson Hole, Wyoming. She received a Bachelor of Science and Teaching degree from Ithaca College in upstate New York. Though semi-retired, her many passions keep her energized and ever curious. Ilene spent much of her life exploring Yellowstone ecosystems on foot and horseback. When a severe horse accident changed her life, she found new ways to let Nature feed her soul, and her writing. When not mentoring the children that she drives to and from school for the Teton County School District, she can be found in Yellowstone with her camper and spotting scope. Ilene can be reached at: P.O. Box 331, Wilson, WY 83014, USA.

PRACTICE:
TAKING A WALK ON THE WILD SIDE

- Dress appropriately to be out-of-doors for at least an hour.
- Bring an adequate supply of water, pen, and journal.
- Select a location where you can both walk on a nature trail and step off the trail to wander in the surrounding area (Note: it is against the rules in some local parks to leave the trail. Please respect local provisions meant to protect you and the natural environment).
- Recommendation: Let someone know where you are going and when you plan to return.
- Upon arrival, practice "*Connecting with Nature*" page 55, or any other activity that will enable you to fully tune into the landscape.
- Spend at least a quarter of your time walking along the nature trail. Notice what your attention is drawn to and what thoughts and emotions are present.
- Journal your observations of both the inner and outer landscape.
- Wander a bit further on the trail and then select a location to wander off the trail into the woods. Notice how your thoughts and emotions shift.
- As you walk forward "introduce" yourself to the natural landmarks and take mental note of their individual characteristics—just as you would when you meet a person for the first time.
- Proceed to explore this natural area for as long as time permits, taking time to journal your observations and insights when you are inspired to do so.
- Return along the same path, "acknowledging" each of your landscape features as your make your way back to the trail. What do you notice about each of them and

about yourself as your return?
- Once back at the trail, journal your observations.
- Repeat the practice often, each time allowing yourself to go a little further from the trail and/or into an area that you have not explored previously. Notice how your ability to become increasingly "intimate" with the nature world influences your relationship with people.

PRACTICE:
SITTING QUIETLY

- Dress appropriately to be out-of-doors for at least an hour.
- Bring an adequate supply of water, pen, and journal, and a cushion or chair to sit on if you so choose.
- Go to a place in nature that you will be safe and uninterrupted. This location might be just outside your home or school or in a remote wilderness setting.
- Recommended: Practice "*Connecting with Nature*" page 55.
- Sit down on the ground and allow your mind to clear.
- For at least an hour, sit quickly and listen to the sounds around you.
- Notice when emotions and, perhaps, memories arise.
- If you find your mind wandering, focus your attention on a specific sound and begin again (You can also repeat the "*Connecting with Nature*" exercises).
- At the end of your observation period, journal your observations. Pay attention to the level of detail of your observations—for example, your ability to notice difference in the distance, direction, and the qualities (level, pitch, tone, tempo, etc.) of each sound.
- Repeat often, noticing how it becomes even easier to "tune in" to the natural sounds.

WOLF TRACKS INTO THE WILDERNESS

Adam Gall

The two words, "Selway" and "Bitterroot," give me chills. Those words conjure up smells, sounds, sights, and tastes that, either combined or focused on individually, are almost too much for me to put into words. Nevertheless, I can tell you of a love story between this incredible land, which stretches across central Idaho and western Montana, and my lucky self.

I have no family ties to this wilderness. What binds me to it is much deeper in my opinion. I had never been in or around it or even heard of it until 1997, when I was hired as a wildland firefighter by the U.S. Forest Service. In four day's time, not knowing anything about the place where my new job was located, I quit my part-time positions, bought a plane ticket, told the folks where I was heading, and flew from Grand Rapids, Michigan, to Missoula, Montana.

I first fell in love on Highway 12. As I crested Lolo Pass and saw the headwaters of the incomparable Lochsa country and the Selway-Bitterroot Wilderness before me, I felt a spark ignite inside and a hotness pulse through my blood. That spark, fueled by wildness, became a fire that burns within me to this day.

The stretch of rugged country you see from the Idaho side of the pass nearly put an end to the Lewis and Clark expedition, and the explorers themselves. I imagine that what they witnessed of the land, however daunting, gave them inspiration and a sense of awe. Today it is difficult, perhaps impossible, to avoid having your heart taken in by the beauty of it. Huge, sprawling mountains are sculpted with voluptuous ridges of pine and fir. The mighty Lochsa River, born from innumerable creeks merging into one, can cause any human soul to tremble. Wildlife still abounds and strengthens one's sense of kinship, respect, and even humor.

Traveling down river with the truck window open, the fresh, soft smell of new cedar soaked into my body. While the lives of the early settlers of this land were no doubt more challenging and perhaps void of some of the fanciful emotions we enjoy today, I believe they knew that stirring, as did the fur trappers before them, and the people of the Nez Perce Tribe before any other human. Although portions of this country have been drastically altered since these first peoples walked across the rugged ridges, on that day I could still engage in a relationship with untamed lands hardly touched or tainted by humans. That was, and still is, fascinating to me.

I think it is fascination that, in part, fuels love. For me, the fascination of this country is held in my desire to achieve a total intimacy with its wild places and all that makes it wild. With intent and time, you can learn how the elk travel the land, on which ridges lightning triggers the death-and-life-giving fires, where and when huckleberries grow fattest, from which pools trout will rise and for what source of protein, and how you could trap marten, coyotes, or wolves in the wintertime, if you had to. Learning these fascinating secrets makes my heart beat faster, almost the same way the heart quickens during an impassioned moment with a lover.

It was Superbowl Sunday, 2000. Friends were all around, drinks were flowing, good food was stacked a mile high and the pre-game commercials were starting up. I have the ability to enjoy all of these things, but that afternoon I found myself called by something more enticing; the clear blue sky, freshly fallen snow, and the sun as it slinked ever closer to the western horizon, teasing the evening. I slid quietly out the side door and drove, just a few miles, down river.

Large sections of the Lochsa were totally iced up and blanketed with several feet of snow. Under these conditions, game can travel slightly easier then their usual trek up steep, heavily forested mountains. The river was a labyrinth of snaking trails etched into the snow by deer and elk. Coyote tracks emerged from the trees. Marten and fisher prints, with their characteristic mustelid hops, traveled and intersected the labyrinth. I strapped on my snowshoes, hoping to catch a glimpse of something wild before dark also left its mark upon the river.

One snowshoe, I don't remember which one, softly creaked with each step, announcing my presence as the pastel tones of the winter sunset grew more intense and deliberate. Despite the noise, I soon came upon a few whitetails. Pleased by the quickness of the encounter, I decided to shoe up a little closer. They were transfixed, staring collectively in one direction, but it was not towards me. I followed their gaze over to the north bank into the timber. I saw nothing but trees.

Nevertheless, what was invisible to me caused a couple of deer to break away from the others and high-step through the snow, down river and across to the other side. It was so silent. Not even the river was audible. In this silence, the remaining deer stood, now visibly nervous, as if they were waiting for their bodies to make up their minds.

Glancing back at the timber, I registered motion. The movement was not that of a deer, but of something else, and I felt myself instinctively straighten. I walked toward the ribbon of forest some 75 yards away. A bald eagle flew overhead. The remaining deer bolted in the direction of the first to flee. What were they aware of that was so veiled to me?

A black wolf loped out of the timber with a light, child-like gait. It moved to the center of the river and stopped, gazing at the whitetails' distant vanishing point. I could see it panting. Thirty seconds passed. Then the wolf took up its seemingly innocent trot in the direction of the deer, leaving me heart struck.

This was the first wolf I had ever seen, or better stated, experienced. I snowshoed down river to where the deer, and later the wolf, had stood. The beautifully complicated, yet simple, relationship between interacting species was summed up right there atop the frozen Lochsa River. As my heart pounded with excitement, disbelief and wonder, I felt insignificantly small, yet larger and more alive than ever before.

A thought crossed my mind—follow the tracks.

But I didn't, and I still dream of that possibility in the way that some people dream of traveling through constellations, or sailing across oceans. I had been swelled up with wonder, a strong wonder. I had surrendered to the spell of fascination. It wasn't the wolf *per se* that I had just fallen in love with, but rather the idea of what wildness it represents, and the role it plays in that big country.

My inquisitive desire aroused questions that made me eager to see and do more. And as I pursued answers, the wolf became my guide into an ever deepening relationship with the wild. What does a wolf see that I don't? How does it perceive its surroundings? How does it use the land to help its cause? What makes it stop, or pick up the pace, or head left instead of right? What scents does it tune in to, or choose to ignore? What would it feel like to experience its existence? Could I follow its lead and slip into the wilderness, materializing only when I wanted to be seen?

Spring ensued and my longing to become a wildlife biologist surpassed my need to be a firefighter. I spent one season as a volunteer and four more as a paid biologist with the Nez Perce Tribe of Idaho, working on the Wolf Recovery Project. Through the work, I learned a great deal about wolves and their ecology, and came to know a good majority of Idaho's topography intimately.

Although the Wolf Recovery Project had many facets, there was one aspect in particular that I did not anticipate. There was, and still is, a "human recovery" taking place as a result of increased human interactions with the wolf, and I find this very intriguing. I believe the wolf's presence offers us the opportunity to rethink our idea of, and relationship to, true wilderness. We are foolish to assume we can control wild places, yet people still try to tame the wilderness, and time and again they find themselves humbled by its ageless ways. To me, the wolf epitomizes the essence of wild, reminding us that the wild, in its various forms, refuses to be domesticated, which I believe is a fantastic thing.

While observing wolves coexisting with humans, I came to understand even more fully how Nature calls attention to the need for wild places. She is ever attempting to remind a sprawling, dangerously-consumptive human society of the power and fragility of their natural surroundings, as well as its own humanity.

The wolf I had seen on the Lochsa that winter evening was a member of the Big Hole pack. In my recollection, it still looks at me. Perhaps, I think, he or she is still trotting through the backcountry of the Selway-Bitterroot, or, heck, maybe it's over in Oregon, waiting to be "officially documented." Yet, many of my specific wonders about that wolf and wolves in general have been replaced by more restless questions—can and will humans continue to inhabit and be inhabited by wild places?

Aldo Leopold once said that the key to intelligent tinkering is to keep all the parts. Can we still have a true wilderness—one with all the parts? Are the gifts of true wilderness enough to merit its existence? Without hesitation, I say yes; knowing true wilderness is an essential part of what it is to authentically live the American dream.

And so, I hope that by returning the wolf-part back to Earth's natural systems, I have helped keep the fascination, heart, and exploration of the wilderness alive. Because the encounter with that black wolf, I feel more in tune with the natural world, as well as self-aware. I believe that given the opportunity to experience wild places, anyone can feel that inner spark and know what it is to be in love.

Adam Gall was a U.S. Forest Service firefighter, a wolf biologist for the Nez Perce Tribe and a high school science teacher. Currently he and his wife are irrigating and running some gardens. He may be reached at P.O. Box 873, Paonia, CO 81428, USA; agall7@hotmail.com.

PRACTICE:
TRACKING

- Dress appropriately to be out-of-doors for at least 1-2 hours.
- Bring an adequate supply of water, pen, and journal. If you'd like to be able to identify the tracks, bring an animal track field guide (See the *Resources* section, page 135, for suggestions).
- Go to a place in nature where you are likely to find animal tracks: the muddy bank of a creek or pond, a nature trail, along the beach, or in the snow, etc.
- Recommendation: Practice "*Connecting with Nature*" page 55.
- Choose a set of tracks to observe and follow. Practice the art of "*Talking a Walk on the Wild Side*," page 64 to keep from getting lost.
- Begin to follow the tracks while imagining you are the animal and asking yourself the following questions:
  o What was the animal likely to have seen that you would not normally notice?
  o How might it have perceived its surroundings?
  o How would it have used the land to help its cause?
  o What might have made it stop, or pick up the pace, or head left instead of right?
  o What scents might it have tuned in to, or chose to ignore?
  o What does it feel like to "experience" its existence? What emotions do you experience? What thoughts are present? How does your body feel?
- Continue the process until you can no longer track the animal or run out of time. If you still have time but have lost the trail, choose another set of tracks to follow and repeat the process.

- Record your observations and insights in your journal.
- Repeat the process often and notice how your tracking ability and intuition grow.

CARARA'S SEDUCTION

Erick Vargas

I was born and raised among coffee bushes, living my childhood under the erroneous belief that Costa Rica was a huge coffee plantation at the foot of massive volcanoes. During school vacations, which corresponded to the coffee harvesting season, I spent most of my time—half playing, half working—in the coffee fields. Other kids and their families were there too: participating in the harvest of our "golden grain" was considered a public duty. Even today, coffee is a major source of work and pride in my small country. Some might even say it provides the roots of our prosperity.

My parents' beliefs, schoolbook lessons, and grandmother's stories also contributed to my less than accurate understanding of Costa Rica and what it meant to be Costa Rican. My mother and father grew up believing that the "montaña," as the tropical rainforest was called, was an enemy to be conquered. For their generation, wealth and wellbeing were the product of the honest labor of farmers and stockbreeders who toiled on lands they had raped and pillaged from the forest. Future possibilities were measured in downed trees and burnt fields.

As young school children we were taught about animals from Africa and North America—lions, zebras, and bears. Not so far from the school yards, diverse and abundant wildlife still roamed the remaining patches of thick rainforest. But these animals were given no mention and thus lurked out there unknown to me for many years.

My grandmother was born close to the turn of the 20th Century in a Costa Rica filled with valleys and mountains much more natural that the ones I inherited. She used to tell me stories about the terrible "tigers" and "lions" that came out of the woods to prey upon small children. For a long time I thought Grandma's stories were pure fantasy, meant to entertain and restrain—every kid knew these animals lived in magical lands far from ours. But years later I learned that Costa Rica's peasants call the puma "lion" and the jaguar "tiger" and that these large cats have always inhabited our wild places. My astonishment was immense, as was the new respect for my grandmother's stories.

Perhaps I was blessed to live my youth at a time of great contradictions for Costa Rica. I found myself called at an early age to figure out who I was and what I believed in. The government ruling my country was, at the time, schizophrenic. On one hand, the country was experiencing, even inviting, the highest deforestation rates in all of Latin America. Simultaneously, foresighted leaders were working against the odds to establish what would become one of the greatest national park systems in the world.

Costa Ricans were truly in a race against time, and we felt it. We talked much about it too. During my teens, teachers offered us many opportunities to learn about our biological diversity and the risks posed by its rapid loss. Although much of the world might have considered us poor, I began to recognize a wealth beyond compare. Thus as a young man, even before I had personally experienced Costa Rica's untamed nature, I made a choice to make a difference—for my people, my country, its wildness, and my soul.

* * *

I awoke at daybreak, taking my first morning breaths in a humid room belonging to Carara National Park's dilapidated ranger station. Carara's deep lushness rises from a tamed sea of pastures and citrus and tuber plantations. She is a wild land, the legalized embodiment of what stirs a man's longings, and his fears. Carara lies alongside the Pacific like a reclining woman, stretching from the dry forest of the North to the moist rainforest of the South.

I had come to Carara to become a park ranger specialized in tourism. The government was going to pay me to build an intimate relationship with this land and to invite tourists to look upon her natural beauties.

Breakfast time was announced by hound-like bellows high and deep in the forest. A male howler monkey, perhaps hundreds of meters or even a few kilometers from our station, was declaring his intent to be known.

I ate, then headed for the trail eager for my first date with Carara's forests—the raw material that would resource my new work responsibilities. As I entered the forest, I was met by a delicate and omnipresent fragrance wafting to me from large piles of dry leaves accumulated under trees of impressive stature. No perfume could ever draw my attention more fully, no matter the wearer. And no manufacturer could hope to duplicate the odiferous work of the fungi, bacteria, millipedes and other soil creatures that voraciously worked the litter into compost, returning precious nutrients to the earth.

My first physical relationship was with the trees. They stood tall and erect, like immense towers born out of a knight's tale of valor. Some were straight and round. Others, like elegant ladies in waiting, wore plush skirted trunks buttress roots that serve to anchor the tree to the ground, making it firm and strong against tropical winds.

I gazed into the canopy and felt awed, nearly overwhelmed, by the number of plants growing thickly upon the branches. The sun was lead actor and these many orchids, bromeliads, ferns, cacti and begonias formed the audience, competing for the best seats to enjoy the staging of light. This was no event meant to entertain—those plants use sunlight to produce their food and it is easier for them to capture it in the canopy than to struggle and compete for it in the dark understory.

Far in the distance I heard a raucous croaking. It had none of the delicate, tonal qualities of our native frogs. As I urged my body down the trail, the sound and I grew closer together until I could actually feel the presence of the performers somewhere in the canopy. I was bewildered. Above my head I saw only branches and a multitude of green hues that colored every corner of the immense forest.

I decided to leave the trail and very cautiously walked some twenty meters into the vegetation. The croaking reached a near-deafening volume. Then, as I reached the foot of a tall corozo palm, I saw them: four scarlet macaws feasting upon fruit hanging in enormous clusters. The birds' feathers shone a deep and brilliant shade of red, contrasting with yellow and blue at the wing. For a few seconds, one of them looked down and examined me with as much curiosity and wonder as I looked up at her.

Scarlet macaws ruled the skies during pre-Columbian times. In less than a generation, "modern civilization" destroyed most of their natural habitat and limited the species to a few isolated protected areas. Fortunately, a small population finds Carara a sanctuary offering food, nesting habitat, and protection from poachers.

And suddenly my mind's eye turned from the trees to gaze inward. The forest doesn't just offer up its services to the animals and plants. It reaches out to us, humans, as well! I had known this in theory, of course, for a long time. But now, now I actually felt the connection between the birds, the forest, and my personal well-being. I felt the connection between the forest's identity and my sense of self. Simply put, I awakened to an understanding of inner- and inter-connectedness, realizing each facilitates the other. The forest is a water factory that enables us to start each day with a refreshing shower. It is also the source of timber for building our homes and furniture. It is a filter that purifies the air we breathe. It is the source of food on our table. The forest sustains our physical needs. But above all this, it is a sacred place. It is a sacred place that opens us to the sacred within us.

In the temple of Mother Nature, my life—and my life purpose—expanded to encompass the forest and its inhabitants in all directions, my heart and soul were infused with a feeling of communion, and I began to pray. I prayed not to the conventional god of my parents but to the Universal Law that permeates everything. I prayed to that Law in the embodiment of Carara as an earthly goddess. And with deep gratitude, I vowed to dedicate my life to preserving Nature's gifts and to sharing my deepest insights with my fellow countrymen.

I returned to the trail only to leave it again at the crossing of an unhurried and shallow stream. Like a child joyously breaking the rules, I boldly waded in, hiking boots and all, and began to explore. Who was here to share in the baptism of my re-birth? The crystal clarity of the pristine waters revealed intimate details—colorful rocks of different sizes, tiny fish, shrimp and a few crabs. I watched a ringed kingfisher make a determined dive into a small pool, masterfully catch his silver prey, and carry it back to a branch for consumption. Further along the river, the clay soil had been stirred making the waters opaque. Very likely, wild peccaries had been wallowing in a refreshing mud bath just moments before my passing.

I again returned to the main trail and headed back to the station. My progress was quickly interrupted by a highly venomous, fer-de-lance snake. He was coiled mid-trail, either awaiting an absent-minded mouse or simply resting placidly, I could not be certain. That extraordinary and misunderstood creature awakened in me a sense of respect and reverence. To many cultures he is the mythic symbol of life and fertility and to Carara he was perhaps a cherished lover.

With her mixture of scents, shapes, textures, and colors, Carara seduced me, too, that day. I would court her and pray to the spirit of her unabashedly for two more years. Walking into the forest of her once and again, I explored her every corner and became ever more intimate with her abundant diversity. Meanwhile, fully knowing she was not for me alone, I worked to create incredible visits for her many other suitors.

* * *

Eventually, life led me to new places and experiences, and what I learned from Carara helped me contribute to the conservation of other public and private protected areas. Throughout the years I have had the privilege to admire mountainous cloud forests and paramos in the highest peaks. I have sailed through quiet, emerald-reflecting canals and rafted in copious white water rivers. I have walked on endless beaches of black volcanic and white coral sands. I have assisted scientists with their studies of plants and animals as they searched for new ways to use them sustainably. I have shared with indigenous communities and local farmers who love the forest and have long had their ways to benefit from it without destroying it. I have joined along other tour guides to explain with great pride the role of a tiny insect in the survival of a gigantic tree. I have witnessed a wonderful change in the values and behaviors of most Costa Ricans, a people now largely aware of its biological treasures and who are eager to contribute to its conservation.

With deep sorrow, I have also witnessed the falling of forests for the making of banana plantations, and the transformation of crystal clear rivers into urban puddles of stinky muck.

I have witnessed the power of people to alter our planet, and my heart is with those who believe that it is possible to live a fulfilling life on this earth, based on natural rules and cycles, without the need to irreversibly destroy it or transform it.

Sometimes the fragrance of the fallen leaves emerges from nowhere and overwhelms me all over again. In these moments I feel more than ever that I can make a difference. I invite the seduction and dream of a better relationship for us all.

Erick Vargas is an environmental consultant and professional speaker working at national and international levels on issues related to biodiversity conservation, ecotourism, and sustainable development. Thanks to a Fulbright-CAMPUS Scholarship, he completed a B.A. in History at Louisiana State University. He then received an M.Sc. in Ecological Tourism from San José-based Latin American University for Science and Technology. In 1993, he became the Ecotourism Coordinator for Carara National Park. Following that position, he dedicated three years to training young men and women from rural communities as nature guides. From 1997-2005, Erick worked at Costa Rica's National Biodiversity Institute, INBio, as the Training Unit Coordinator. He is a certified Master Practitioner in Neuro-Linguistic Programming (NLP) and member of Ecos Systems Institute's faculty. Erick can be reached at: erickvc@racsa.co.cr.

PRACTICE:
AWAKENING TO THE FOOD-LAND CONNECTION

- You will need access to a library and/or the internet.
- Select one of your favorite natural foods or meal ingredients, maybe it's a fruit or a vegetable, or even chocolate (cacao).
- Use the internet and/or reference books to find out how and where that food is commonly grown. What kind of natural environments have been cleared for its production? What kind of pesticides or fertilizers are routinely used? Are there some production methods that are more environmentally-friendly than others? What companies engage in these practices, or what certification programs exist that provide labels on products grown with these practices? What local and international environmental organizations are working to support sustainable production?
- Based on the information you have gathered, make a conscious decision to purchase these foods from producers or through certification programs that support sustainable agriculture, or what is termed ecoagriculture.
- Support environmental organizations that are working with the agriculture industry and local farmers to reduce the impact of agriculture on natural systems and human health.

Resources: Learn more about connecting your values with your purchase decisions through Conservation Value, see: http://www.conservationvalue.org. For more information on ecoagriculture, visit: http://www.ecoagriculturepartners.org.

LEARNING FROM OUR ELDERS:
TEACHER TREES
Tina Fields

Ode to a Linden Tree

Dear Guest, sit down beneath my leaves and take your rest.
  The sun will not strike you there, I do insist,
Though it beat from its noonday height, and its direct rays
  Should pierce such scattered shade as a tree bestows.
There, a cooling breeze is always blowing from the field;
There, nightingales and blackbirds their tuneful tales unfold.
  It's from my fragrant blossom that the timeless bees
  Take the honey, which later ennobles your lordly feasts;
Whilst I, by my soft murmurs, can easily contrive
That gentle sleep should overtake the unsuspecting fugitive.
  It's true, I bear no fruit; but in my master's eyes
  My worth exceeds the richest scion of the Hesperides.

-the Squire of Czamolas

I was considered a weird kid. When I was nine, my
frizzy, dark auburn hair was far from the stylish straight-
and-blonde. I didn't care what my clothes looked like or
whether they even matched, let alone what label adorned
them. I was far from athletic. I wore glasses. I used big
words, and understood their meanings. While other kids
gossiped and invented small tortures for fun, I read, drew,
and daydreamed. As an only child, I was poorly versed in
mind games, and usually lost out long before I even realized
the teasing had begun. When I grew up, I wanted to be a
philosopher and a witch.

All of this added up to the bleak reality that I didn't have
many friends. Most of the time that was actually fine, as I
enjoyed the freedom that came with solitude. Fortunately, I

found myself to be pretty good company. But there were also challenges. Like many only children, I didn't need to seek acceptance through pack conformity. (I knew it was a lost cause.) Sadly, such a hermit-like attitude can also activate the playground-pack dynamic in which mistrust and fear of difference manifests as cruelty toward those who somehow find a sense of individuated authenticity. There were times when even my closest friends would turn on me in an attempt to keep their tenuous places in the schoolyard pecking order. When provoked, I wouldn't fight with them; instead, this taunting made me turn even more solitary. The people-centered life felt hard, and I often turned to the more-than-human world for companionship.

In the park across the street from my childhood home, a pine and a maple welcomed me with open, low branches. The pine tree was enormous. I'd climb the rungs of its ladder self, rising as high as I could go, and cling to its wide but flexible trunk as the wind swayed us back and forth. It felt ecstatic to ride the wind like that, especially in a high storm. Upon my descent, I'd be covered with pitch and pitch-glued pine needles. My poor mother tried to freeze the hardened gluey gunk out of my hair and clothes with ice, only to give up in disgust time and time again, and hack it out of my lion's mane with scissors. I endured all this with equanimity, as my tree time made me feel completely wild and at peace.

The maple was smaller than the pine and oozed no pitch, so it was my most frequent tree-of-choice. However, it was also harder to scale, so I'd only go as high as its second branch. This was a comfortable branch; just the right shape for me. I could sit upon it for hours, and I would, too, especially when life seemed particularly hard.

Being aloft held its own surreptitious pleasures: People would walk by down below, and never know I was perched above them, overhearing everything. Giddy, I learned that most people rarely think to look up. By staying silent and observing other people's behavior, I began to awaken to the dark holes in my own awareness, and decided to try to notice everything. Expanding my vision, I realized as the weeks passed how utterly accompanied I was in the world. Life, motion, spirit abounded everywhere. I began to wonder how much I was missing because I had not been looking with truly aware, open-minded eyes.

After particularly difficult days at school, I'd enter the maple in the way some church goers step into confessional boxes. Climbing up, I'd wrap my arms around it, lay my cheek against its rough-barked trunk, and tell it my woes and dreams. Sometimes I'd cry. Day after day, week after week, for a couple of years, I wept my sorrows into that tree.

And then one day, the tree spoke back.

This might sound crazy or like a make-believe story, but it really happened. I was so surprised that I nearly fell off the limb. I didn't hear its voice with my ears. Rather, the message came in a word and picture combination that manifested in my mind, yet was not my own. The message didn't feel like it originated from within me; the words didn't sound like mine. In my gut, I knew they came from this tree. It was a full-blown couplet of image and speech, bearing a message I remember and live by to this very day.

The maple advised, "Be like the linden tree. It bends and bends in every wind, yet its roots go down deep, deep, deep."

I had never even heard of a linden tree before, much less had any idea what one looked like or how it behaved. It would not be until twenty years later, while living in Europe, that I would meet my first linden tree and feel as though I'd been reunited with a long-lost, much beloved relative.

The ancient Greeks and the Slavs believed the goddess of love abided in the linden tree. Other Europeans, especially the Poles, regarded linden trees as symbols of divine power, family, faith, and valour. When Christianity arrived in the region, the linden became the tree of the Blessed Mother. In many a folktale, the Blessed Mother hid among the tree's branches, waiting patiently to reveal herself to children.

The linden's white blooms are fragrant, making them a favorite of bees and beekeepers. Bees produce wax for candles, honey for mead. Laws often protected the precious trees. To cut down a linden meant bad luck, perhaps even bringing tit-for-tat death to self or a family member. Such was the reverence for lindens.

The maple's message to emulate this unknown cousin reverberated in me from that moment forward. The world was suddenly full of far greater possibility than I'd ever before imagined. A tree can speak? It's conscious? What else is happening that I haven't noticed or participated in? I set out and within—on a mission of curiosity and deeper exploration.

Before that day, my parents had taken me camping many times. Every time, they had exhorted me to "look at the beautiful scenery!" but I ignored them, preferring to read a comic book. No more. Suddenly the world was so much more than mere stuff. I went from being surrounded by dead matter to being part of a community of aware beings with desires, thoughts, and volition. I began to closely observe other animals, plants, rocks, clouds, and to consider how best to serve our collective well-being. I became interested in mysticism and spirituality, and began to explore comparative religions, looking for human wisdom about relating to the numinous in everything.

Whatever happened in the purely human realm took on far less import. Personality glitches or opinions of me, whether coming from other kids or my own self-doubt, seemed fleeting and insignificant. I was determined to be kind, but to also put human interactions into a much larger context. Like a tree, I stood in a forest of mystery and hope. And, as soon as I stopped caring what anybody thought of me, I attracted good friends and became popular.

Trees, each in their own way, have been my great teachers. They cradled me, brought me into contact with elemental excitement, and woke me up to the living world in all of its intense spiritual mystery and innumerable dimensions. They initiated me as a participant in life instead of a reluctant observer.

The influence of trees has made me a better, wiser, and more aware animal who lives fully in an expanded world sprouting with possibility, fun, and friendship. I will honor these elders of other species as long as I live. I hope that they will continue to teach us all and that we youngsters along the evolutionary scale will keep actively seeking out ways to listen.

Tina Fields taught interdisciplinary environmental studies, animistic philosophy, and community living skills at the college level for the past nine years, first for Lesley University's outdoor-based Audubon Expedition Institute, then for New College of California's North Bay MA program in Culture, Ecology, & Sustainable Community. She holds a PhD in East-West Psychology, with a specialization in Ecopsychology. Her work mainly focuses on the vital questions of how to foster respect for the more-than-human world, and how to find joy instead of deprivation in shifting to planetary-life-sustaining behavior. Tina is also an accomplished visual and performing artist, community song-leader, bioregional naturalist, scholar/practitioner of shamanism & Celtic earth-based spirituality, DIYer, and incorrigible punster. She lives in a 470-sq.ft. cottage in Sebastopol, CA, and can be reached at: tfields8@yahoo.com.

PRACTICE:
TREE CLIMBING

- When was the last time you climbed a tree? Explore those memories. If you have never climbed a tree before, what stopped you?
- Dress appropriately to be out-of-doors for at least an hour and to enable you to climb trees. Bring an adequate supply of water, pen, and journal.
- Go to an area with trees that have branches low and strong enough to climb. These trees might be in your yard or in a wilderness area. (Note: it is against the rules in some local parks to climb trees. Please respect local provisions meant to protect you and the natural environment).
- Practice "*Connecting with Nature*" (Parts 1-4, page 55).
- Select a tree to climb and do so, being attentive to your safety. Choose a branch that will support your weight and sit on it for at least a half hour.
- What do you notice from this perspective—both around you and within you? Record your observations in your journal.
- Turn your attention to the tree, noticing the details of its bark and leaves and limb structure.
- Practice "*Connecting with Nature*" (Part 5, page 55). Pay close attention to what comes into your awareness.
- Recommendation: Practice "*Story Telling with the Spirits of Place*" (page 46) with the tree.
- When your time is up, carefully descend from the tree.
- Recommendation: Offer the tree a prayer tie (page 132). Journal your observations.
- Repeat the practice often, building a relationship with the same tree and/or with other trees. What wisdom do you learn from them individually and collectively?

PRACTICE:
NATURE AS CULTURAL GUIDE

- You'll want to have a pen and journal handy, as well as access to a library and/or the internet.
- For at least one side of your family, determine your bloodline's national/regional origin(s) and cultural heritage as far back in time as you can.
- Using the internet and books, explore the spiritual practices of this culture(s) and time period, paying close attention to the role of nature. Explore the following questions:
  o What types of plants or animals were considered sacred?
  o What practices existed to honor these plants and animals?
  o In what ways were these plants and animals protected?
  o Where there any plants or animals specifically associated with your family name (such as on family crests). (Note: there are several websites that will enable you to use your family name to search for information on geographic and cultural history and family iconography.)
- Consider what roles these plants and animals have played in your life. Are there any similarities to their historical role? Pay attention to the role these plants and animals play in the future, as well as in your dreams.
- Journal your observations.

Resource: The National Geographic Society's DNA Ancestry Project will enable you to trace the roots of your ancestral bloodlines. For more information, see: http://www.dnaancestryproject.com/.

ONE LITTLE CREEK

Gale Lucas

I wasn't some crazy environmentalist kid trying to save the world; I was protecting one little creek that is special to me. I was guarding the lives of creatures that I called by name and sheltering a waterway that I knew even better than the back of my hand. Over the five years that I visited Mill Creek, I developed an intimate knowledge of the place. I could follow every bend in the serpiginous path of this cas-cading creek with my eyes closed. I could smell the earthy musk of the soil, feel the refreshing breeze, and taste the es-sence of springtime. I heard the water sing and the birds rejoice. To me, Mill Creek is not just one little creek.

The first time that I found Mill Creek, I discovered my Self. Standing on the bank of the meandering stream, I watched the clear, crisp droplets surge between two zigzag-ging walls of dirt, mud, and sticks. I heard the rush of life flowing by as the water trickled effortlessly past my feet. The forest spoke to me, alive with the rustling of life imbued by the winding creek. I could see the tiny creatures that dwelled at the creek bottom scurrying about in their day-to-day lives, as we humans do, unaware of others' presence. Their move-ments scattered the water ever so slightly in the direction opposite the creek's natural flow. They moved among the finely feathered algae and soft silky wet moss that lined the rocks, coating them like a plush green carpet. The pungent smell of this flora was nothing like the saccharine sweet scent of store bought flowers—it was more delicate to my senses, not sharply aromatic, but soft and natural. The musky smell filled the forest and took me back to a time where untamed nature was all that existed. My mind was lost without a care, transported by the smells and sights and sounds that sur-rounded me. I was 12 years old.

Wading into the creek's waters took me the next step, freeing me to be one with all that encircled me. I felt the rhythm of the creek, resonating in its unending flow. I glimpsed my Self in the "mirror" of that crystal running water, seeing not my physical reflection, nor my ego. I saw my authentic Self, my soul. Peering back at me was the Self that is the water, the canopy of trees it feeds, the murky silt and speckled pebbles at the creek bottom, and even the mayfly larvae embedded within that rock-strewn base.

A momentous change had occurred within me, the first and most profound of my personal mystical, natural experiences. At the edge of Mill Creek, I had come to know the world in a completely different way. I had awakened to my connectedness to everything around me from my human neighbors to the sweet fresh air, the birds flitting about, and even the wiggly brown worms in the dirt bank of the creek. Unintentionally replicating Christian baptism, I had re-immerged from that water a transformed person.

While I had always enjoyed being in nature, until I stepped into the waters of Mill Creek, I had not realized that a piece of land could be like a relative. Intellectually, I knew that we depend on the natural world for sustenance. I was aware of our fate if we did not respect Nature. Yet I had not realized that we can be one with the trees; that we need Nature in order to experience a sustained happiness and peace, a sense of harmony and tranquility in life. Before encountering the spirit of Nature at Mill Creek, I was trapped within my own mind and body. Locked inside the shallowness of my own flesh, I could not experience what it felt like to be free—to be my Self.

Spiritual rebirth gives one another try at life's great journey, a second chance at a more meaningful life. Just a change in one's perception allows shifting from a self-centered life to existence in the eternal—it must feel akin to leaving the isolation of prison for a life among the free. My life path began with this discovery, communing with one little creek.

What would I be without this creek? Would my soul be as content, would my heart be at ease if I had not found the power radiating from that natural space?

Two years later I had the chance to give back to this piece of land that had changed my world. As the creek had "saved" me, I worked to save it. Addressing the Prison Siting Committee and the audience in attendance, I surprised that room of more than a thousand people. They no doubt expected me to say how dangerous it would be to have a prison near my middle school. But I had not come to protect our neighborhoods and schools. I was there to save one little creek.

I told them that Mill Creek was one of the few areas left for wildlife. I explained that, as our once-quiet town grew into a bustling suburban city, all of the wild creatures were pushed into pockets of undeveloped, natural land. I illustrated that one of the largest and most fragile of these wild spaces was the riparian area of Mill Creek, the proposed site for prison placement. I warned that a beautiful lush little valley housing unique northwestern species from owls to trout would literally be demolished and covered by asphalt. It would be imprisoned, and sentenced to death.

At the close of my speech, I told the audience, "This place I am trying to save has a lot of power—the power to break us out of the self-concerned prison of daily life." I said that a piece of land has the power to shape a life, and Mill Creek had shaped mine. In return for this gift, I wanted to defend the birds and trees and mayflies that are my brothers and sisters—a part of my Self.

As I spoke, I realized that each and every plot of natural land is a precious gift. Mill Creek is a piece of land that has touched so many lives. I am just one example. And Mill Creek is just one example of the many special places that deserve our protection. If every crazy environmentalist kid had one sacred place to save, what a world this would be. I walked back to my seat. It felt good, right, to give my all to protect this special creek from becoming a wasteland of concrete and barbed wire, and human isolation.

When Mill Creek was designated a protected green space, I was elated. The place that helped me to find my Self is now secure, forever a stronghold of free souls.

So I say "thank you" to the creek. Thank you from me personally, for all the gifts you have given me. I thank you, Mill Creek, for all of those who have been touched by you, for those who enjoy you now and for those who will have the opportunity to find themselves in you in the future. You, Mill Creek, have a lot of power.

Gale Lucas is a fourth year graduate student at Northwestern University, having received a psychology degree with a religious studies minor from Willamette University, the oldest university in the West. She is pursuing a PhD is social psychology, and then plans to teach students and conduct research in a university setting. Prior to college, she was involved in the Student Watershed Research Project, a program in which students study the health of local wetlands and report their findings to the city. She plans to continue to experience and help protect our natural world and always to return to her sacred place of power, Mill Creek. Gale can be reached at: Northwestern University, Department of Psychology, Swift Hall, 2029 Sheridan Road, Evanston, IL 60208-2710, USA; g-lucas@northwestern.edu.

PRACTICE:
PARTICIPATING IN LOCAL CONSERVATION

- Use your local newspaper and phone book to identify opportunities within your community to work on conservation issues (contact your local land use planning commission and conservation organizations, for example).
- Volunteer as much time as your schedule will permit to protect natural places in your area.

THE SENSE OF LIFE

Elena Galante Marcos

Every story has a beginning, and the beginning of this one takes place in Salamanca, Spain, where the Castilian Plateau guards thousands of secrets and where it is still possible to find the landscape I fell in love with.

On the Castilian Plateau the fields fade into the horizon. It is a vast prairie, with a unique ecosystem: the *dehesa*, a savanna-like Mediterranean land that hosts the holm-oak tree. I have never seen similar fields, or at least none that could bring the same feelings up within me. Its colors are ochre and blue; the ochres of vegetation burned by a sun too accustomed to its own presence and the blues of a clear summer sky that floods everything with light.

Once in a while, it is possible to glimpse the bell tower of a distant church emerging from the fields. Each of the wall stones in those churches has been a story keeper for that land for more than 500 years. Each stone remembers the passing of countless flocks of sheep tended by lonely shepherds, and nesting swallows building little hanging baskets of clay and reed under the roof eaves during their short, seasonal stay in Spain. Each stone has felt the weight of the winter snow and scorch of summer's heat.

In the summer, the fields give off a very special fragrance. The aroma, I venture to guess, is a unique mixture of pollen and sun-filled sky. It is a scent that is warm and soft. It is a fragrance that smells like sunset, like Castile, like village, like heat and tranquility.

My first visit to the *dehesas* resides in my memory like a living picture filled with sensations, smells, sound, and images. I was seven, and my brother was five. I remember stepping into an open field and, as I looked across the vast hillside, suddenly knowing what it is to be wild and free. We ran and skipped beyond the calling edge of parental voices.

Almost immediately, I came to cherish the holm-oaks, magnificent trees with wide, outstretched, embracing branches along the Castilian prairies. They were strong and easy to climb. Some could support a rope swing and giddy child. A variety of bushes, blooming cactuses, and the silhouettes of fine, fierce bulls kept the company of holm-oaks.

Bulls grazed as if they owned the *dehesas*, as if they knew they were one of the best-known symbols of Spain. I remember being greatly impressed that day by one particular bull. His impeccably black hide glistened in the sun, and his thick, strong neck appeared incredibly sturdy, like the holm-oak branches. I imagined swinging from it like a noisy, human cowbell. His shiny eyes rested deep within his head, like dark, deep, mysterious wells. Was he looking through me? I wondered. Never before had I seen such a beautiful and proud animal.

Although Spain's bulls are famous for their fierceness, they were tranquil that day and quite indifferent to my presence. Time stood still as I gazed upon them, filled with feelings of admiration and peace. Few images bring me as much joy as that of a fighting bull resting its hard-tested body next to a weathered holm-oak.

This was to be the first of numerous visits to the *dehesas*. As the daughter of entomologists, I spent many weekends walking through the fields of Salamanca looking for insects with my parents and brother. Our mission was to find beetles and hoverflies; the first were inevitably linked to bull dung, and the latter were to be found upon flowers scattered throughout the fields. Upon each visit, the *dehesas* opened my heart a little more, until I fell in love with all of Nature.

My mother, a biology professor, specialized in flies. She would give me a butterfly net and a warning to refrain from catching insects close to thorny plants. To me, hoverflies were like bees that did not bite. I learned that if I looked closely at the insect and saw it flying, stationary in the air-like a hovering helicopter—it was hoverfly, and not a bee. My mother regularly reminded me that many different plants reproduced thanks to hoverflies; pollen sticks to the flies' bodies and is then transferred around the field as they pay their visit from one flower to the next.

Although using the butterfly net was great fun, I found it more even effective and pleasurable to use my ears to study Nature. When I heard a cricket singing, I would follow the sound until I found its hiding place. Then, using a blade of grass, I would coax it out for a meeting of souls. Sometimes I liked to run into the bushes and listen, quietly, to the voices of the plants and animals. They always had something to say; I could hear the cicadas shake their wings to soothe the tremendous heat, and the sky-clever swifts and the swallows chittered and chattered as they grabbed insects from the air. When I couldn't hear anything, I would listen to the silence of the field, which is never absolute.

Dung beetles held a particular fascination for my brother and me. Perhaps it was because our father looked upon our play proudly. Or, perhaps, it was something deep within our cells that called us to the beetles in the same way the beetles called him. We loved to poke through piles of bull dung with sticks, searching out the beetles. Each time one appeared, we would celebrate and spend countless moments watching it construct and then roll balls of bull dug, often many times larger than itself. My father used to say that without those beetles, the *dehesas* would certainly disappear; the dung beetles worked everyday to clean it up. "Somehow," he said, "they are like the road sweepers of the countryside." What lucky children we were to be able to be so intimate with Nature.

At mealtimes we would select an ideal shade tree to sit under, with rocks to sit on. We would make straws out of hollow grass blades and remark that food tastes better out in the open. Sometimes, after lunch, I would fall asleep on a blanket, hoping to pass unnoticed by the sultry heat. I remember how mysterious the fields looked as I crossed the threshold between day and dreams.

At the end of each visit, no matter how long the nap, our bodies were always completely exhausted. Yet, in spite of the tiredness, I often refused to leave. Instead, my eyes and ears traveled the horizon with the black clouds of noisy swifts announcing sunset.

When I finally did agree to depart, I would take a deep breath before climbing into the family car: country air was healthy for us, my mother used to say, so I always made sure to inhale the invisible magic and fragrance of the *dehesas*.

My days in the Castilian countryside taught me how to hear, observe, smell, read, and feel Nature in my skin. They also taught me that, when surrendered to, one's passions can sustain the needs of the physical body and the soul. Now, every time I discover a new landscape, I search for the special fragrance of the place and when I find it, I invite my memory to gently return to the smooth and vast *dehesa*. I smell the warm vegetation under the holm-oak and I become seven, wild and free, all over again.

Elena Galante Marcos was born in Spain, but currently resides in Costa Rica. After graduating in Advertising and Public Relations from the University of Alicante, Spain, she moved to Costa Rica with the hope of combining her expertise in communications with her passion for Nature. She enjoys studying the interface between biodiversity research and ecotourism development, and uses her advertising and communications expertise to make technical findings available to the public. Elena manages a Spanish cooperation project on the Costa Rican–Nicaragua border (www.proyectoriofrio.org), and is pursuing a master's degree in Sustainable Tourism Management. Elena can be reached at egalante@inbio.ac.cr.

PRACTICE:
FRAGRANCE AND MEMORY

- Dress appropriately to be outdoors for at least an hour.
- Bring an adequate supply of water, pen, and journal.
- Go out-of-doors to a location that will enable you to take an uninterrupted walk and/or to sit quietly.
- Once there, relax (Option: Do the "*Connecting with Nature*" practices on page 55), close your eyes, and take in a deep breath through your nose. What do your smell?
- Explore the following questions: What images does the smell or combination of smells bring to mind? What emotions do they stir? What memories? How old were you when these memories were formed and what role have those experiences had in shaping your life?
- Journal your observations.
- Move to another location and take in another deep breath with your eyes closed. What do you smell?
- Explore the same questions and repeat the entire process as time permits.
- Repeat the process often and notice the degree to which fragrance "anchors" our emotions and our memories.
- Explore how your life would be different if the sources of those fragrances were no longer a part of the natural environment.
- Find ways to bring the fragrances of the natural world that open your heart and mind into your home and office–through aromatherapy, potted flowers, or simply an open window.

Sustenance

Ellen H. Brown

While other girls in high school were going wild over cute boys with long hair and tattered jeans, I was falling hard for my first love: the glistening, sumptuous mysteries of the natural world. Like many love affairs, mine took me by surprise. The catalysts were an unassuming and bespectacled science teacher named Mr. Haskett, and what many would consider a nondescript swathe of green in an otherwise urban area called the Shaker Parklands. But there was nothing unassuming about Mr. Haskett's enthusiasm for Nature, and nothing pedestrian about the Shaker Parklands, a magical oasis on the fringes of Cleveland, Ohio, and its inner-ringed suburbs. In Mr. Haskett's ecology class, we took weekly "nature walks" and the world, literally, came alive for me and within me. Each time we ventured into Nature, I felt such a sense of wonder and reverence, such a sense of peace. The world became an enchanting place, as I learned the names of the beings with whom I share Earth. Beautiful beings with exotic names that delighted my tongue: Names like trout lily and skunk cabbage, jack-in-the-pulpit and bloodroot, cinquefoil, and jewelweed. Over time, I also came to know the wise old beech trees and sycamores that had held steadfast to the earth through lightening strikes and thunderous winds, and I came to love them. I became privy to the intricacies of marsh, stream, and woodland, and realized that the power to hurt or help these beings was in my hands.

One hike literally whet my appetite for the natural world. As we strolled, single file, along the trail that autumn morning, breathing in the crisp, leafy air, Mr. Haskett stopped periodically. Looking up and down, he introduced us to a variety of nuts and edible plants. Some were native to the area and others had been brought to America by early settlers who had many uses for them. The dandelions we often view as undesirable weeds, for example, have delicious leaves when newly sprouted. And when we came upon a black walnut tree, Mr. Haskett paused. "These are the most delicious nuts," he said, picking one up and peeling off its musky, green husk. Deep within the tough, woody seed lay the soft nutmeats.

At the hike's end, Mr. Haskett gave us that our next assignment; we were asked to create a "dish" made with at least one wild ingredient found in the Shaker Parklands. Our creations were to be shared with the class in a sort of natural food feast. In an instant, I knew what I would make: banana walnut bread!

A week later, I hiked again into Shaker Parklands, returning to the black walnut tree. It was tall and lanky, and its dark grey bark was mottled with lime green lichens—no two alike. Each main branch was fingered with spindly smaller branches reaching in a myriad of directions. Small, golden yellow leaflets carpeted the thickening forest floor. I reached down among the leaves and collected several of the large, blackening nuts. I made sure to leave plenty there for the local wildlife, and wondered what animals would follow in my footsteps. A variety of wildlife, including chipmunks, squirrels, white-tailed deer, and even woodpeckers, will eagerly devour black walnuts.

If I do say so myself, the bread was delicious. Though it's been nearly three decades since I baked that bread, I can still taste the bittersweet richness of those nuts. I understand why Native Americans and early settlers prized them, and gourmet pallets hold them in high regard today.

That experience expanded my appreciation for the natural world. It fed my body and soul, and ultimately inspired my desire to preserve and protect the Earth's precious resources. Though Mr. Haskett never once told us that we had a duty to become caretakers of Earth, I felt this truth as a deep knowing in my own body.

In college, with an enthusiasm for Nature well seeded

within me, I planned to study botany or zoology and to become a naturalist or park ranger. Back then, I envisioned myself as the great protector of the natural world, a sort of pint-sized (I stand about five foot tall) Mother Earth. But sadly, I allowed my fear of the "hard sciences"—mostly chemistry and physics—to domesticate me. In the end, I settled for a major in journalism and a career as a writer.

Through the years, though, my love for all beings, big and small, has continued to grow. With each season that passes, I find myself wandering more often through the woods and wetlands for comfort and inner sustenance. Recently, when my husband and I were in the market for a new old home, we decided to plant our roots in the place my heart calls home, a place close to the Shaker Parklands. We travel to the Parklands—alone and together—several times a week. The land is a touchstone that provides me with great comfort and joy, and I feel thankful that this sanctuary exists amid the chaos of what is commonly called "civilization."

Along the shores of the Shaker Lakes and through the woodlands, I have befriended the beeches and geese and great blue herons. Sometimes it feels like there are no barriers between us. I take Nature in, cultivating an ever more intimate relationship with the natural world. If you open up, Nature can nourish you—in so many ways.

Ellen H. Brown is a nature lover, wellness coach, and avid writer who makes her home in the Greater Cleveland area, among the sycamores and maples. She currently runs a communications consulting business and a wellness coaching company, Wellness Journeys (http://www.wellnessjourneys. com). Through her business and volunteer work, Ellen hopes to awaken others to the wonders of the natural world, just as Mr. Haskett did for her years ago. She can be reached at ehb@ehbcommunications.com or ebrown@wellnessjourneys.com.

PRACTICE:
A TASTE FOR NATURE

- You will need access to a library and/or the internet.
- Make a list of four or five of your favorite foods.
- Research of origins of these foods, tracing them back to their wild relatives (i.e. specific plant or animal species).
- Determine:
  - The region of the world or country in which they originated.
  - The type of ecosystem their wild relatives inhabit or inhabited.
  - The current status (e.g., rare, common, etc.) of the wild relatives.
- Next time you prepare a meal, contemplate the diversity of wild plants and animals that are connected to your ingredients.
- Consider what would happen to the food supply and diversity of available foods if these wild relatives went extinct.

FLOW

Chev Kellogg

I awoke needing to see the river.

The strength of her calling and my deeply echoed long-ing puzzled me as I sat upon a shoreline rock, cloaking my-self in the Kaweah River dawn. A cold breeze chilled my skin, bringing up goose bumps and questions.

My rational mind nagged, "What are you sitting here for when you could be nestled in a warm bed? What if someone notices? You'll look stupid."

Indeed, I had a full day of research ahead of me and was feeling a bit conflicted about courting the river while the others, all professional scientists, slept soundly in the hotel room. Like a teenager who had snuck out from his parents' house for a forbidden date, I contemplated how I was going to explain my behavior if I got caught.

There are voices within me that worry about my wild-ness. They fervently whisper, "Don't do that. Act like ev-eryone else." They scold, "You are wasting your time. Go do something productive."

On that morning I let the thoughts and cold bite deep enough to become emotions. I could feel every irregularity of the rock and my nervous ego press uncomfortably into me. Struggling, I moved my legs forward and back, swayed my torso, and shifted my weight away from the particularly sharp and edgy spots. I must have looked like I was having a slow-motion seizure. Life can be like this.

Gradually, the rush of the river began to take hold of me. In watery, tinkling roars, alternately cajoling and insistent, she, like an unquenched lover, demanded my full attention.

Out of the foggy memory of other times spent in Na-ture's hold, I remembered why I needed to be there that morning. I was alive. There was nothing more important to do. The aches, chills, and hurry-thoughts that fill too much of my domesticated life left me alone with the river. My soul flowed out to touch her.

The Kaweah has one of the smallest watersheds of any river in the United States, draining out of Sequoia National Park right through Three Rivers, California. It's small for a river, maybe twenty feet across where I had settled. Just a few miles downstream Terminus Dam traps the high gradient rush popular with kayakers in a lake frequented by anglers. Below the spillway, orange groves rise up along the banks quickly enough to surprise you. Other men have had their way with her in other places, in other ways.

Where I sat, the river flowed over, around, and through sand bars, willows, boulders, sycamores, cobbles, grasses, and me. Evidence of the flow's long outstretched, steady hand was everywhere. Even the largest rocks were well rounded. The water had left no edges. She knows how to caress.

Leaving my perch, I walked away from the active channel, back through time, to find sand. The gritty mass clung to my wet fingers in a kaleidoscope of yellows, reds, browns and oranges that confused my eye. I hadn't expected to be confounded by sand, but there I was staring at a handful of Earth's ancient body in the faint light of a chilly morning. I laughed. It was a soft laugh, escaping through a smile, nothing anyone would hear over the river, but a laugh nonetheless. Holding a handful of the Sierras in my hand overwhelmed my common senses. I rubbed the sand back and forth across my palm, and felt it pass coarsely between my fingers. I continued to laugh as a way of saying, "I get it." This must be how the riverbed feels as the Southern Sierra Nevada slips by her, bit by bit, washing downhill with the Kaweah.

This sand is one of the major reasons for Sequoia National Park. The sandy soil from glacial erosion and weathering of the park's crystalline rocks cradle the roots of the giant sequoia, *Seguoiadendron giganteum*. These soils, combined with large amounts of precipitation dropped on the mountains by moist air from the Pacific, create the conditions needed for survival of the ancient trees. The oldest trees have helped keep that soil in place for more than 4,000 years, but even these giants can't hold on to every grain. Some has slipped down past their roots into the Kaweah and through my fingers. Nature has a hard time containing herself. The desire to flow is an ancient force.

Painting the remaining sand onto my pant leg, I took my seat again by the river. Every wave, ripple, and rock stood out in rich form and essence, more brightly than what could possibly be lit by the morning sun. Willow saplings and mature sycamores leaned downstream. Young or old, the river flow treats bank life with the same constancy of attention.

Debris in branches above my head told me that the river stretches out her arms often enough to fully embrace these trees. I wondered if both tree and river eagerly awaited the winter melt and the deepening of their relationship.

Was debris a sign of courtship? I wondered. High flows wove it into branches like the littering of love notes, while lower flows placed it around trunks like an offering or a promise of things to come. I started to sense the nature of the relationship between the river and land. It was eternal and ephemeral, constant and ever changing.

Looking into the river, I was suddenly looking into a mirror of thoughts and could sense the flow of things within. The rocks, sand, plants and water were all on their way from somewhere to someplace else. They were all on the move, but weren't traveling alone; my thoughts and feelings went with them and they brushed against my hopes. I knew in that moment that I was part of the flow, and as the river headed to the ocean, I wondered where I would end up someday. Though completely alone on the river bank, I knew that I had found solitude rather than isolation. In that moment, I knew deeply that people are not separate from their environment, but are part of it. The relationship between the river and land includes me. As a scientist, I know about interconnectedness intellectually, but it's only upon visiting the wild places within and around me that I truly feel interconnected.

As I sat there, I imagined myself as part of the flow of time. If I sat there long enough, the atoms of my body would be replaced with those that flow out of the Sierras. First the carbon, oxygen, and hydrogen would be replaced, then, if I stayed yet longer, iron and calcium, until I became fully a product of that place. How long would it take? I wondered. What is the turnover time of a person?

Or maybe, I thought, becoming a place is more a matter of a change in perception rather than molecules. What is the spiritual turnover time of a person? In that place, on that morning, it was pretty fast.

It was my need for relationship, for deep connection, that drew me out that morning, and it is what keeps drawing me out, what makes the bits of untrammeled country so precious to me. I need these places to know who I am, to find out who I can become, and to figure out how to be true to my own nature and live in the world.

At some level, I feel the places also need me. They need my thoughts, my presence, and my love. They need my protection from the actions of others too far physically and emotionally removed from the land to realize the worth of it. On mornings like the one spent by the river, I am reminded of my long-term relationship with Nature and vow to let gratitude flow, undammed, from my heart forever.

Chev H. Kellogg has a doctorate in Biological Sciences from
The University of Notre Dame where he studied plant ecology and soil chemistry in restored wetlands. He has been
an environmental engineer, combat engineer platoon leader,
plant ecologist, climate change researcher, and a mathemati-
cal modeler, and jumped out of planes and helicopters with
the Special Forces. The author of several articles on wetland
and terrestrial ecology, he has done ecological research in
Sequoia National Park, California, the Upper Peninsula of
Michigan, and many points in between. He currently con-
ducts water quality research at the Minnesota Department
of Natural Resources and is active in local watershed management activities. You can contact Chev at: 990 Jameson
St., Saint Paul, MN 55103, USA; chevkellogg@gmail.com.

PRACTICE:
ENGAGING IN THE FLOW

- Dress appropriately to be outdoors for at least an hour.
- Bring an adequate supply of water, pen, and journal, and cushion or chair to sit on if you so choose.
- Go to a stream or river and find a place where you can sit, uninterrupted, along the bank.
- Once at that location, employ the "*Connecting with Nature*" practices (page 55) or other methods that you use for getting grounded, centered, and focused.
- Take a comfortable seat at the water's edge.
- Turn your attention upstream and notice what comes into your awareness.
- Explore these questions: What aspect of you is traveling or trying to travel upstream? By what means is it making progress? Is it fighting against the current or steadily moving forward?
- Journal your observations.
- Turn your attention downstream and notice what comes into your awareness.
- Explore these questions: What aspect of you is traveling or trying to travel downstream? By what means is it making progress? Is it going with the flow or holding on to partially submerged debris out of fear? Fear of what?
- Journal your observations.
- Look across to the other bank and notice what comes into your awareness.
- Explore these questions: What kind of flowing body of "water" exists between where you sit now and the next "place" you need to be in your life—the next shore? Metaphorically, is it a quiet, meandering creek or a high velocity river strewn with boulders and rapids? What do you need to do to get to the other side? What is your first

step and when can you take it?
- Journal your observations.
- Repeat this process anytime you feel "stuck" and outside of the "flow of life."

HOPE FOR A WOUNDED PLACE

Rebecca L. Buckham

Standing at the trash-lined edge of the Sweetwater Marsh that January afternoon, I wanted nothing more than to escape southern California. It was a new year, but not much had changed. Overhead, the busy freeway transitioned north, away from the wetland habitat beneath its cement overpasses, and away from me. I covered my ears to block out the frantic roar, but could still hear its mad rush inside my head. Brushing past tumbleweeds, I felt green glass from broken beer bottles crunch between my shoes and the hard ground. Caught among the bristling weeds, plastic grocery sacks whipped the air. Shoelaces and cassette tape reels tangled in the bushes, and an old sneaker sat with its dirty tongue pulled out, rubber sole dry and cracked. Smelling of seawater and sewage, a gust of wind rattled the tumbleweeds and I turned my nose in disgust. I felt as if the brown afternoon haze had entered my nostrils and crept into my unhappy soul.

"This," I bitterly thought, "is my place." But I did not love it.

The marsh, just miles from where I grew up, gets its name from the less-than-lovely Sweetwater River. Bound by sloping concrete walls, the river is caught between two freeways, one moving east and the other running west. On either side, shopping centers and parking lots receive and discharge the freeway's speeding cars. And, sprawling in all directions from the stores and cars, are houses—house upon house upon house, each with a patch of grass for a yard and three cars parked on the asphalt outside. Here, where I stood frowning, this concrete-lined river dumps into this forgotten marsh, depositing grocery bags from those stores and plastic bottles from those houses before seeping into the San Diego

Bay.

Like all wetland habitats, the Sweetwater Marsh is a fragile ecosystem, vulnerable to heedless human activity. Though ecologically critical, it is easily overlooked, and has suffered at the hands of urbanization and industrialization. Absorbing the impact from storms, the mudflats and estuarine channels serve as a buffer between the ocean and land. They have also served as a buffer against the tide of human activity, and the damage lies visible in the garbage and foaming sewage collected among the grasses and in the bends of snaking streams. To many people, this marsh appears as it did to me that day—a wasteland with little inherent value.

On that first day of the new year, I imagined that the marsh and I felt much the same—tired, hopeless, and consumed by the voracious appetite of more powerful things. Things like "The American Dream" and "Suburbia," and the bigger-is-better mentality of a place obsessed with glitz and glamour, sexy Hollywood stars, and multi-million-dollar homes.

When I listened to my father reminisce about adventures in the woods behind his childhood home in Pennsylvania, I envied him. I never rode my bike to "town," I never built forts in the shady parts of secret woods, and I never fished for trout with homemade lines on a Sunday afternoon. I had memories, sure, but no one reminisces about duplexes and chain-link fences. Suburban southern California had stolen something from me, and I was angry.

Fuming, I picked up a discarded water bottle and turned it in my hand. The peeling label boasted of pure mountain springs. I threw it back down to the ground and shouted at the marsh.

"Why try? Why even try!?"

I was, in a way I did not understand and could not explain, angry at this place. I was angry at the freeway, and at the channeled river, and at the marsh that appeared less as a natural habitat and more as a dumping site for industrial waste and household trash. Moving through the grasses, I stepped over rubber gloves, a plastic toy sword, a license plate frame. Styrofoam packing peanuts floated on the surface of narrow estuarine channels winding through the mud. A shopping cart lay half-submerged in water, its rusted bars bent like broken ribs. I felt as if the marsh was angry, too. At any moment I might hear its hard, angry voice.

"What do you want?" it might demand.

"I don't know," I might reply. And then, gesturing towards the marsh and the freeway in the background, "Not this."

"Then why are you here?" A valid question from an angry place.

I kicked aside a rusty, dented can. "Why *am* I here?" I asked myself. I didn't want to be here. And yet I was drawn here, away from crowds of after-Christmas shoppers and "Happy New Year" well-wishers.

A new year means nothing to this marsh; it brings no hope of change. This marsh cannot make a resolution to improve itself. A new year just brings more of the same—the marsh will continue to fill and drain as the tide changes, will continue to collect plastic bottles and Styrofoam cups. The river will continue in its concrete course, and the freeway will continue overhead, and the cars will continue to race by, and the people in their cars will continue to enter and exit the freeway, getting and spending and buying and throwing away.

I sank down onto a thick bed of matted grasses that rustled beneath me like plastic drinking straws. On the horizon, construction cranes were drawn like unfinished outlines in the sky. Behind me, a crowded trailer park spilled down the hill. I wanted to escape. I wanted to close my eyes and, when I opened them again, find myself elsewhere. I felt sick. And yet I remained, struggling to look deeper into the nature of this seemingly hopeless place.

Then, for a brief moment, my sickness became the marsh's

sickness, and I could not distinguish myself from this land-scape. I cried out, but it was not my familiar voice. It was the voice of a wounded, wasted place. My place. It was a lament, and I felt it take hold of me as spirit possesses body. Breath-ing, I felt this spirit enter me like the rising tide enters and fills these wetland rivers. My veins became sinuous marsh channels, my organs sand and mud, my thoughts grasses that moved in the breeze. I wept, and my tears were the brack-ish currents slowly twisting at my feet. I felt then as if I was looking out a window and all of a sudden saw my own re-flection focus in the glass. In that moment, I recognized this wounded place as a reflection of my wounded self.

And so, I found a deep connection with my place. It was not the romantic connection that I wanted, and it was not with a place I found easy to love. Nevertheless, after my encounter with the Sweetwater Marsh that day, I did begin to build an authentic relationship with my place. I began to understand that real love shares in suffering and, ultimately, in healing.

I was drawn to the marsh because I needed to see some-thing real, even if that something was ugly. What I encoun-tered was my wounded self, reflected in a wounded marsh. I realized that I was angry not at this place, but at myself. I could not lay blame on a freeway, or on a littered marsh, or on a polluted river. I could only confront the same self-ishness in me that drives much of human society. Walking through the marsh and sharing in its wounded cries, I saw and lamented the ugliness inside of us all, the ugliness we try so hard to ignore by distracting ourselves at shopping malls and over freeway interchanges.

We need to acknowledge these wounded places. We need to acknowledge them not only on an ecological level, but also on a spiritual level: by experiencing a wounded place, we are reminded of our dis-ease as individuals, and of our dis-ease as a society. We need to look into these places to see our-selves, and in seeing ourselves to be reminded of our power for both good and bad, and in being reminded, to change, and to heal. And so I did, after my January walk through the Sweetwater Marsh, feel hope. This hope, however, was not the passing hope of a new year, but the lasting hope of a changed relationship with my self and with my place.

Rebecca Buckham is a graduate student in English literature at Villanova University. She is devoted to exploring the intersection of Christianity and environmental issues, and tailors her academic work around the concerns of ecocriticism. Her article, "Eden Voiced: Milton's Dialogic Community of Creation and an Environmental Ethic of Partnership," will be published in a collection of essays from the 2005 National Conference on John Milton. Of late, she has enjoyed hiking modest sections of the Appalachian Trail, and loves to compost and watch birds. She can be reached at: 5875 Unit C Reo Terrace, San Diego, CA 92139, USA; rebeccabuckham@gmail.com.

PRACTICE:
THE NATURE OF WOUNDS

- Dress appropriately to be out-of-doors for at least an hour.
- Bring an adequate supply of water, pen, and journal.
- Go to a heavily disturbed "natural area" in an urban setting, or a place in the rural environment that metaphorically seems "wounded" to you (where a forest was clear cut, for example).
- Once at that location, spend a few minutes *"Connecting with Nature"* (page 55) or employing other practices that will relax you and open your mind and heart.
- Choose a place to stand or sit—it need not be comfortable!
- Look around you and notice what comes into your awareness.
- Explore the following questions: What is the nature of the wounds of this place? Are they bruises, gashes, breaks, contusions, etc.? Are they open, scabbed, healing? What caused the wounds and what is enabling them to heal?
- Journal your observations.
- Taking your attention within, continue with these questions: When I look upon these "wounds," or one in particular, what emotions and memories arise within me? What is the nature of the wound(s) that I am carrying? How old was I when they were formed and what were the circumstances? What condition are they in? What has stopped them from healing thus far? What do I need to do now in order to facilitate their healing?
- Journal your observations.
- Turn your attention back to the landscape and wander it, looking for signs of renewal, healing, and resistance.

What can you learn from these processes that will aid in your own inner restoration?

- Journal your observations.
- Repeat the process often, noticing how it becomes easier to let go of your own wounds and invest your energy in healing the land, as well as the human landscape, around you.

RED RIBBONS AND RECIPROCITY

Marlow Shami

Russians once had a thing for trees and red ribbons. To protect yourself from a storm, they believed, you should tie red ribbons around trees. If you wanted to repel the evil eye, tie a red ribbon around a birch. To honor the ancestors, the living gathered together to decorate their homes with red-ribbon-adorned birch branches, which, when later burned, enabled the spirit of the dead to move on. In reciprocity, the dead protected their living relatives.

As a child, I recall tying my father's red necktie around a tree behind my home. He had a closet rack full of neckties and I figured he wouldn't notice if I took one. He didn't.

* * *

The crackling aroma of dry oak leaves underfoot calls me back from an empty place of bewilderment. I start to cry, then laugh, as the white clapboard house I've been trying so hard to live in grows smaller—until, thankfully, it seems to be consumed by dense green foliage. The sounds I make feel red and wrap around the trees, ride the wind, and usher me away from that ill-tempered house.

Once in the forest, where soft invisible eyes keep watch, I know what it is to be at home. I reach my special dwelling place—an exposed, three-chambered bedrock outcropping—and, slide my weary six-year-old body into the womb-like welcome of the stone's interior.

Nestling in, I open all my senses. The wind blows my brown bangs back and scatters a blanket of leaves across the forest floor. I follow the deep, mysterious crevasse downward until I come to an opening. There, I lay face to earth, eyes shut, in a space between a red oak and shiny black birch—a space between hardship and hope. My breath mingles with the soil, acorns, leaves, and tiny wind-broken, lichen-covered branches. The swamp just down the hill is blinking with frogs. A deer cautiously moves through the mud. Cicadas pulsate—first one, then ten, and in another few seconds the whole forest shimmers with their sound. A luminous wave of life flows over, then recedes through me. This is what it is like to be free.

I roll onto my back and sigh as a huge cumulus cloud passes over. The shape of a horse grows out the side; its tail turns into a large snake, which is consumed by yet another horse. This one is running. I break off a small birch stem and scratch the dark outer bark, exposing the bright green inner-skin. I chew it. It tastes like bubble gum. This is what it is like to be alive.

A faded red silk tie wrapped around the black birch catches my eye. The tie was a gift I offered to the tree a few months ago, in the spring. It was my way of saying, "thank you."

* * *

There, on that hillside, I absorbed the healing comfort of Nature. I was an unhappy, confused kid, and that landscape expressed compassion. The numinous touch of the rock's nurturing womb imprinted an inner devotion to reciprocate. So I do, by living a life, as best I can, that mirrors the kinship and respect birthed and embodied by my childhood experiences in Nature.

Forty-five years after making that offering of the red tie to the black birch, I felt called to embark on a pilgrimage of even greater gratitude—to return to the rock as a ritual of thanks.

On that day, the old sugar maples on either side of the street flickered gold and shadow across my windshield. I exited off New York's Saw Mill River Parkway and wound my way to the end of Pine Cliff Road, the passageway to my special dwelling place—which is now, thankfully, an Audubon sanctuary.

I took one of the two parking spaces at the trailhead and followed the boardwalk's meander. The red maple swamp of the 60s had formed a small, very bright algaed pond. I encircled it, mesmerized. The low croak of a bullfrog serenaded red dragonflies zooming with precision on travels to various feeding and sunning spots bordering the pond.

Then, halfway around, I stepped off the boardwalk onto dry ground. An old stonewall caught my eye and my memory. The wall was built in the early 1740s by John Reynolds, a fact the town historian, Gray Williams, provided. It was most likely created in the clearing of land for cow pasture and apple orchards. As a child, rather than keep me out or pen me in, it served as my guide. It led me to the swamp and let me know that my small feet hadn't much further to go to reach my stone sanctuary. I invited the serpentine pile of stones to lead me once again to the sacred site to which I had come to pay homage.

After a few minutes of walking uphill along the southwest side of the wall, a prominent stone form beckoned me from the ridge. I felt the boundary of my consciousness expand, encompassing whatever my attention was drawn to. Within that hillside, shadows wove in variegated currents of branch, leaf, and stone. The forest was imbued with the earthy fragrance of moist soil and decomposing wood and crackling oak leaf, it elicited in me a sense of warm receptivity and equanimity. The feeling settled over me in soft alchemic hues. "Ahhh," I thought. "Here is where it began. Here is where I first felt Nature's healing touch."

Squatting down, I picked up a large red oak leaf and reflected on time and the succession of seasons. Who would I have become were it not for a 1.1 billion year old, white-and-black banded, metamorphic rock of Fordham Gneiss?

"Never mind," I smiled.

 Although the ongoing process of erosion is slowly diminishing this magical outcropping, the intelligence of the natural world that had sustained, mirrored, and comforted me as a child had continued to grow.

The red tie is long gone, now a part of the soil beneath the ageing black birch it once hugged, yet Nature's reciprocity inhabits the land, everywhere. I leaned against ancient stone and reflected upon the moments I've woken up and noticed Nature's consistent invitation to return home—to home in all its forms. I hear it in the owl's late night call, see it in the old white pine stand, and in the glimmering scales of a trout resting beside a smooth, round river stone. The northern lights glowing pink ribbons hold sparks of this force. So too, the power shines in the spots of the fawn, eyes of the bear, and screech of the bobcat traversing the hills of northwest Connecticut, where I now live. These moments scatter like polished gems over the landscape offering up the balm sought by my Russian elders. We are still alive.

I imagine my great-great Russian grandmother gathering up red ribbons with her neighbors, then setting off to anoint each birch on the hillside surrounding her small Circassian village. Returning at dusk, they make a toast, drinking, then passing the Bakhisma in a communal bowl, each holding the shimmering metal container up to the crescent moon with a smile, knowing the land is aware. We are still free.

It's near sunset. Golden mauve clouds streak the western sky. I relax in the memory of red ribbon, forest, sky, and stone—my spirit opens and a soft presence awakens from the inside out. My shoulders soften, my breath deepens, and my fingers gently touch the ingrained landscape of rough stone and sweet birch. There is warmth here. And there is love. Red is the color of love. Now, I am offering myself up to the world.

Marlow D. J. Shami, BFA, MS, teaches ecopsychology through her workshops, writing, and art work. Nature's healing process inspires her life. She lives in the rural Northwest corner of Connecticut with her partner. Her neighbors include bobcat, fox, squirrel, lady slipper, trillium, crow, and Sylvia the red hen. Marlow can be reached at 97 Pie Hill Road, Goshen, CT 06756, USA; marlowshami@sbcglobal.net.

PRACTICE:
PRAYER TIES

- You will need the following: red and white cloth cut into squares swatches (about 2.5 inches per side), twine, loose tobacco, scissors, and a bag to carry these in. (Note: Ideally the cloth and twine will be of natural, organic materials, such as cotton and hemp, and the tobacco will be organic as well.)
- Dress appropriately to be outdoors for at least an hour.
- Bring an adequate supply of water, pen, and journal.
- Go to a treed natural area where you have permission to leave tangible objects. This might be a place on your own property, or a friend's property, or a sacred place honored by members of the community.
- Once at that location, do the "*Connecting with Nature*" practices (page 55) or employ other practices that will enable you to make offerings from your heart.
- Focus your intent on the gift, prayers, and/or blessings that you want to make here. Perhaps it is a prayer on behalf of the place, a friend, or yourself. Maybe it's a blessing that you want to offer up by means of celebration, gratitude, or simply the recognition of natural beauty.
- With one specific intent in mind (and heart), create a prayer tie by placing a small amount of tobacco (a pinch appropriate to the size of the swatch) in the middle of the cloth. Then gather the four corners of the cloth together above the tobacco and tie them together with the twine. Cut the ends of the twine, leaving enough length to enable you to tie the small bundle around a tree branch.
- Select the tree that you would like to honor or partner with in your offering.
- Tie the bundle onto the tree branch, being sure not to

bind it so tightly as to impact the tree's growth.

- Make any other offering to this tree that you feel is appropriate for the role that it is playing in your ceremony.
- Repeat the process for each of the prayer ties that you wish to offer.
- Option: Fasten your prayer ties to each other and place them on the tree like garlands.
- Recommendation: Adopt the tradition of conducting a prayer tie ceremony as a means of letting go of those things (particularly beliefs and behaviors) that no longer serve you (pick one color to represent these) and claiming or inviting in those inner resources and actions that you need to more fully engage in your life mission (the second color will represent these). Select specific dates and/or natural events for your ceremony, such as summer and winter solstice, the full moon, or nature-based holidays practiced by your ancestors (e.g., Beltane and Samhain if of Celtic descent).

Resources

Organizations

Organizations offering wilderness-based retreats, conferences, or workshops intended to foster an intimate and transformative relationship with the land:

Animas Valley Institute
www.animas.org

Center for the Story of the Universe
www.brianswimme.org

DrummingCircles, LLC
www.drummingcircles.com

Ecos Systems Institute
www.ecos-systems.org

Kripalu
(relevance based on particular courses)
www.kripalu.org

Omega Institute for Holistic Studies
(relevance based on particular courses)
www.eomega.org

Outward Bound
www.outwardbound.com

River Drum
www.riverdrum.com

Sacred Ways
www.sacred-ways.org

The River Wind Foundation
www.theriverwindfoundation.org

The School of Lost Borders
www.schooloflostborders.com

Academic Programs

Universities and colleges offering degrees in ecopsychology, the study of the relationship between human well-being and the human connection to nature:

California Institute of Integral Studies
www.ciis.edu

Lesley University's Audubon Expedition Institute
www.getonthebus.org

Naropa University
www.naropa.edu

Northland College
www.northland.edu

Pacifica Graduate Institute
(ecopsychology and depth psychology combined)
www.pacifica.edu

Prescott College
www.prescott.edu

Project Nature Connect (online program)
www.ecopsych.com

Professional Societies

Networking and informational opportunities for professionals interested in the study of the human dimensions of landscape conservation:

The Society for the Anthropology of Consciousness
www.sacaaa.org

The Society for Conservation Biology
www.conbio.org

The Society of Ecopsychology
www.ecopsychology.org

The Society of Human Ecology
www.societyofhumanecology.org

Conservation Organizations

Nonprofit organizations focused on land conservation:

Rails to Trails Conservancy
www.railtrails.org

The Land Trust Alliance – www.lta.org

The Nature Conservancy – www.tnc.org

The National Park Foundation – www.nationalparks.org

The Trust for Public Land – www.tlp.org

The Wildlands Project – www.twp.org

The Wilderness Society – www.wilderness.org

Land Connection as a Way of Life

A declaration of core principles for building a sustainable, just, and peaceful global society:

The Earth Charter Initiative
www.earthcharter.org

Earth-Focused Ministry

One Spirit Interfaith Alliance
(earth-based and more)
www.onespiritinterfaith.org

The Circle of the Sacred Earth
circleofthesacredearth.org

Recommended Reading

Books and literary magazines by authors who explore and celebrate the human relationship with the land:

Magazines

Orion
www.orion.org

The Sun
www.thesunmagazine.org

139

Books

Abram, David. *The Spell of the Sensuous: Perception and Language in the More-Than-Human World.* New York, NY: Vintage Books, 1996.

Ackerman, Diane. *A Natural History of the Senses.* New York, NY: Vintage Books, 1990.

Anderson, Lorraine (ed.). *Sisters of the Earth: Women's Prose and Poetry About Nature.* New York, NY: Vintage Books, 1991.

Blakey, Nancy. *Go Outside: Over 130 Activities for Outdoor Adventures.* Berkeley, CA: Tricycle Press, 2002.

Berry, Thomas. *The Dream if the Earth.* San Francisco, CA: Sierra Club Books, 1988.

Brown, Tom. *Tom Brown's Field Guide to Nature Observation and Tracking.* New York, NY: The Berkeley Publishing Group, 1986.

Brown, Tom. *Tom Brown's Science and the Art of Tracking.* New York, NY: The Berkeley Publishing Group, 1999.

Carson, Rachel. *The Edge of the Sea.* New York, NY: The New American Library, 1955.

Carson, Rachel. *The Sense of Wonder.* New York, NY: Harper & Row, 1956.

Chard, Philip Sutton. *The Healing Earth: Nature's Medicine for the Troubled Soul.* Minocqua, WI: NorthWord, 1994.

Cohen, Michael J. *Reconnecting with Nature: Finding Well-*

140

ness Through Restoring Your Bond with Earth. Lakeville, MN; EcoPress, 1995.

Cornell, Joseph. *Sharing Nature with Children*. Nevada City, NV: Dawn Publications, 1979.

Dillard, Annie. *Pilgrim at Tinker Creek*. New York, NY: Harper & Row, 1974.

Gallager, W. *The Power of Place: How Our Surroundings Shape Our Thoughts, Emotions, and Actions*. New York, NY: HarperPerennial, 1993.

Glendenning, Chellis. *My Name is Chellis & I'm in Recovery from Western Civilization*. Boston, MA: Shambhala Publications, Inc., 1994.

Hart, Roger. *Children's Experience of Place*. New York, NY: Irvington Publishers, 1979.

Hill, Julia Butterfly. *The Legacy of Luna: The Story of a Tree, A Woman and the Struggle to Save the Redwoods*. New York, NY: HarperCollins Publishers, 2000.

Hoffman, Edward. *Visions of Innocence: Spiritual and Inspirational Experiences of Childhood*. Boston, MA: Shambala, 1992.

Kahn, Peter H., Jr. *The Human Relationship with Nature: Development and Culture*. Cambridge, MA: MIT Press, 2001.

Kahn, Peter H., Jr. and Stephen Kellert. eds. *Children and Nature: Psychological, Sociocultural, and Evolutionary Investigations*. Cambridge, MA: MIT Press, 2002.

Kanner, Allen D., Theodore Roszak, and Mary E. Gomes.

Ecopsychology: Restoring the Earth, Healing the Mind. San Francisco, CA: Sierra Club Books, 1995.

Kaplan, Rachel, and Stephen Kaplan. *The Experience of Nature: A Psychological Perspective.* New York, NY: Cambridge University Press, 1989.
Kingsolver, Barbara. *Small Wonder.* New York, NY: Perrenial, 2003.

Leopold, Aldo. *A Sand County Almanac: With Essays on Conservation from Round River.* New York, NY: Oxford University Press, 1966.

Louv, Richard. *Last Child in the Woods: Saving Our Children from Nature-Deficit Disorder.* Chapel Hill, NC: Algonquin Books of Chapel Hill, 2005.

MacEowen, Frank. *The Mist-Filled Path: Celtic Wisdom for Exiles, Wanderers, and Seekers.* Novata, Calif.: New World Library, 2002.

McKibben, Bill. *The End of Nature.* New York, NY: Anchor Books, 1999.

Metzner, Ralph. *Spirit, Self, and Nature: Essays in Green Psychology.* El Verno, CA: Green Earth, 1993.

Mosley, Ivo (ed.). *Earth Poems from Around the World to Honor the Earth.* San Francisco, CA: Harper Inc., 1996.

Oliver, Mary. *Blue Pastures.* Orlando, FL: Harcourt Brace and Company, 1995.

Oliver, Mary. *White Pine.* Orlando, FL: Harcourt Inc., 1994.

Orr, David. *Earth in Mind: On Education, Environment, and the Human Prospect.* Washington, DC: Island Press, 1994.

Plotkin, Bill. *Nature and the Human Soul: Cultivating Wholeness and Community in a Fragmented World.* Novata, Calif., New World Library, 2008.

Plotkin, Bill. *Soulcraft: Crossing into the Mysteries of Nature and Psyche.* Novata, Calif.: New World Library, 2003.

Pyle, Robert Michael. *The Thunder Trees: Lessons from an Urban Wildland.* Boston: Houghton Mifflin, 1993.

Roberts, Elizabeth and Elias Amidon (eds.). *Earth Prayers from around the World: 365 Prayers, Poems, and Invocations for Honoring the Earth.* New York, NY: HarperCollins, 1991.

Schama, Simon. *Landscape and Memory.* New York, NY: Vintage Books, 1996.

Sewall, Laura. *Sight & Sensibility: The Ecopsychology of Perception.* New York, NY: JP Tarcher, 1999.

Snyder, Gary. *The Practice of the Wild.* Washington, D.C.: Shoemaker & Hoard, 2004.

Sobel, David. *Beyond Ecophobia: Reclaiming the Heart in Nature Education.* Great Barrington, MA: The Orion Society and the Myrin Institute, 1996.

Wilson, Edward O. *Biophilia.* Cambridge, MA: Harvard University Press, 1986.

Wilson, Edward O. *The Naturalist.* New York, NY: Warner Books, 1995.

Whyte, David. *Fire in the Earth*. Langley, WA: Many Rivers Press, 1999.

Whyte, David. *Where Many Rivers Meet*. Langley, WA: Many Rivers Press, 1998.

Singles

Opportunities to meet singles interested in the out-of-doors:

Green Singles
www.greensingles.com

The Science Connection
www.sciconnect.org

For Children

Resources for introducing children to the magic of the land:

Educational Programs

Project Learning Tree
www.plt.org

Project WET
www.projectwet.org

Project WILD
www.projectwild.org

Magazines

144

Nature Friend Magazine
www.amazon.com

Ranger Rick Magazine
www.nwf.org/kidzone/

Books

Baker, Jeanne. *Where the Forest Meets the Sea.* New York, NY: Greenwillow, 1988.

Cherry, Lynne. *The Sea, the Storm and the Mangrove Tangle.* New York, NY: Farrar, Strauss, Giroux, 2004.

Cherry, Lynne and Mark J. Plotkin. *The Shaman's Apprentice: A Tale of the Amazon Rain Forest.* Orlando, Florida: Harcourt Brace, 1998.

Cherry, Lynne. *A River Ran Wild.* Orlando, Florida: Harcourt Brace, 1992.

Cherry, Lynne. *The Great Kapok Tree: A Tale of the Amazon Rain Forest.* Orlando, Florida: Harcourt, 1990.

Fraser, Debra. *On the Day You Were Born.* Orlando, FL: Harcourt, Inc., 1991.

Johnson, Donald B. *Henry Hikes to Fitchburg.* Boston, MA: Houghton Mifflin, 2006.

Johnson, Donald B. *Henry Climbs a Mountain.* Boston, MA: Houghton Mifflin, 2003.

Romanova, Natalia. *Once There Was a Tree.* New York, NY: Dial, 1989.

Russel, Naomi. *The Tree.* New York, NY: Dutton, 1989.

Simon, Carly. *Midnight Farm.* New York, NY: Simon and Schuster Books for Young Readers, 1997.

Wood, Douglas. *Grandad's Prayers of the Earth.* Cambridge, MA: Candlewick Press, 1999.

Television

Zoboomafoo
(for preschoolers)
http://pbskids.org/zoboo/

Kratts Creatures
www.krattscreatures.com

Eco Systems Institute

Home is a name, a word, it is a strong one;
stronger than magician ever spoke, or spirit ever
answered to, in the strongest conjuration.
　　　　　　　　　　　—Charles Dickens

Ecos is Greek for "home." Ecos Systems Institute (ESI) is a doorway through which individuals can more fully come home to themSelves, their community, and the greater family of things of which they are a part. ESI employs a co-creative process to generate publications and programs that inspire eco-logical awareness, expand heart and mind consciousness, and, ultimately, foster Earth-honoring practices and traditions.

ESI is a non-profit organization founded by ecologist and ecopsychologist, Dr. Jamie K. Reaser. For more information, visit: http://www.ecos-systems.org.

About the Editors

Jamie K. Reaser, PhD believes in the potential of the human spirit. She is a practitioner and teacher of ecopsychology, nature-based spirituality, and various approaches to expanding human consciousness, as well as a conservation ecologist, wilderness rites-of-passage guide, poet, writer, artist, and homesteader-in-progress. She is the author or editor of more than 100 publications, including *Bring Back the Birds: What You Can Do to Save Threatened Species*. Her photographs, illustrations, and poems appear in books, magazines, and calendars. She makes her home at Ravens Ridge Farm, 85 magical acres in the Blue Ridge Mountains of Virginia. Jamie can be reached at Ravens Ridge Farm, 1207 Bull Yearling Road, Stanardsville, VA 22973, USA; ecos@nelsoncable.com. More information on her work can be found at: http://www.jamiekreaser.com.

Susan Chernak McElroy is a New York Times bestselling author, storyteller, and teacher. She has written numerous books, including the bestselling, *Animals as Teachers and Healers*, and has been featured in a host of anthologies that explore the connection between humans, animals, and the wild. Susan offers lectures and workshops on cultivating deeper appreciation for the wild within and without. She now resides in Bloomington, Indiana. Her website is http://www.susanchernakmcelroy.com.

Printed in the United States
144262LV00001B/1/P

9 780979 924637